Advanced Introduction to Artificial Intelligence in Healthcare

Elgar Advanced Introductions are stimulating and thoughtful introductions to major fields in the social sciences, business and law, expertly written by the world's leading scholars. Designed to be accessible yet rigorous, they offer concise and lucid surveys of the substantive and policy issues associated with discrete subject areas.

The aims of the series are two-fold: to pinpoint essential principles of a particular field, and to offer insights that stimulate critical thinking. By distilling the vast and often technical corpus of information on the subject into a concise and meaningful form, the books serve as accessible introductions for undergraduate and graduate students coming to the subject for the first time. Importantly, they also develop well-informed, nuanced critiques of the field that will challenge and extend the understanding of advanced students, scholars and policy-makers.

For a full list of titles in the series please see the back of the book. Recent titles in the series include:

The Sociology of Work
Amy S. Wharton

Marketing Strategy
George S. Day

Scenario Planning
Paul Schoemaker

Financial Inclusion
Robert Lensink, Calumn Hamilton and Charles Adjasi

Children's Rights
Gamze Erdem Türkelli and Wouter Vandenhole

Sustainable Careers
Jeffrey H. Greenhaus and Gerard A. Callanan

Business and Human Rights
Peter T. Muchlinski

Spatial Statistics
Daniel A. Griffith and Bin Li

The Sociology of the Self
Shanyang Zhao

Artificial Intelligence in Healthcare
Thomas H. Davenport, John Glaser and Elizabeth Gardner

Advanced Introduction to

Artificial Intelligence in Healthcare

THOMAS H. DAVENPORT

Distinguished Professor, Babson College, Fellow, MIT Initiative on the Digital Economy and Senior Advisor, Deloitte's AI Practice

JOHN GLASER

Executive in Residence, Harvard Medical School and Lecturer, Wharton School, University of Pennsylvania, USA

ELIZABETH GARDNER

Independent Journalist

Elgar Advanced Introductions

 Edward Elgar
PUBLISHING

Cheltenham, UK • Northampton, MA, USA

Published by
Edward Elgar Publishing Limited
The Lypiatts
15 Lansdown Road
Cheltenham
Glos GL50 2JA
UK

Edward Elgar Publishing, Inc.
William Pratt House
9 Dewey Court
Northampton
Massachusetts 01060
USA

A catalogue record for this book
is available from the British Library

Library of Congress Control Number: 2022938786

ISBN 978 1 80088 808 1 (cased)
ISBN 978 1 80088 810 4 (paperback)
ISBN 978 1 80088 809 8 (eBook)

Printed and bound in Great Britain by TJ Books Limited, Padstow, Cornwall

Contents

Tables

About the authors

Thomas H. Davenport is a Distinguished Professor of Information Technology and Management at Babson College, a Visiting Professor at Oxford University's Saïd Business School, a Fellow of the MIT Initiative on the Digital Economy, and a Senior Advisor to Deloitte's AI practice. He has written or edited more than 20 books. The most recent is *The AI Advantage* (MIT Press). He has contributed more than 300 articles to *Harvard Business Review, MIT Sloan Management Review,* and many other publications.

John Glaser is an Executive-in-Residence at the Harvard Medical School. He is on the faculty of the Wharton School at the University of Pennsylvania and the UTHealth School of Biomedical Informatics. He is a former senior vice president of Population Health at Cerner Corp. He was chief executive officer of Siemens Heath Services and served as chief information officer at Partners HealthCare (now Mass General Brigham).

Elizabeth Gardner has spent most of her journalism career covering healthcare, with an emphasis on business issues, quality of care, and the application of information technology to clinical problems. She began as the IT columnist for *Modern Healthcare,* and has been a contributing writer for *HealthLeaders* and *Health Data Management.* She has written for the US News *Best Hospitals Guide* and numerous other publications and is a developmental editor for NEJM Catalyst's peer-reviewed journal *Innovations in Care Delivery.*

Preface

On the morning of January 1, 2032, Tony Ambrosio woke up with (he thought) the mother of all hangovers. He didn't remember much from a raucous New Year's Eve party the night before. His wife was visiting their grandchildren, and the absence of her normal controls on his behavior led to some extremely unhealthy activities.

Tony tried to go back to sleep, but something—it turned out to be his watch—was beeping at him, loudly. He struggled to focus on the watch screen, thinking that he'd inadvertently set a wakeup alarm. But it was blinking a different kind of wakeup call entirely: "HEALTH INDEX WARNING: STROKE OR HEART ATTACK. Click crown for large screen health monitor." Tony tapped the crown and his touchscreen TV turned on. It was filled with bright red warnings:

- A drop of thirty points overnight in his predictive health score
- High arterial blood pressure
- Low blood oxygen
- High carbon monoxide in his blood, possibly from fire or excessive cigarette smoke
- Rapid heart rate with likely arrhythmia/atrial fibrillation
- High LDL cholesterol level.

The system asked Tony if he had recently experienced confusion, changes in vision, or weakness. His shaky finger clicked on all three: symptoms he had attributed to excessive alcohol consumption.

The screen flashed "LIKELY DIAGNOSIS TRANSIENT ISCHEMIC ATTACK (TIA)": a small stroke (the system explained) that could be a precursor to a large stroke. The system recommended he take three aspirin immediately, which fortunately he had on hand. Going back to the diagnosis screen, Tony read, "Northwestern Google Cigna Medical Center has dispatched a mobile medical facility (MMF) to your home at 2240 Thornberry Road. It will arrive in six minutes. Click here if you can answer the door." Tony clicked that he could, and before he could even brush his teeth, he heard a vehicle enter his driveway.

Tony was a bit dazed as the emergency medical technicians led him into the MMF, an emergency room on wheels. One EMT gave him a rapid blood test to confirm the stroke and listened to his neck with a stethoscope. They removed his watch and wedding ring and put him into the mobile MRI machine. A neurologist visited the MMF via a telehealth screen, reviewed the images from Tony's MRI results that had been flagged by the machine's AI algorithm, and confirmed a "mini-stroke" that probably originated in his carotid artery. The neurologist prescribed an aspirin regimen for the next several days and had the EMTs apply a sensor patch to collect electrocardiogram data over the next week. They showed Tony how to sync the patch with his smartphone to transmit the data, and made sure the linkage was working. "We'll let you know if you need to come into the hospital," the neurologist concluded. "You'll be hearing from our LifeBot care coordinator with a consult on diet and exercise, to help protect you from another one of these, or a bigger one. Lay off the booze and for God's sake quit smoking." The screen went dark. Tony was "discharged" from the MMF just as his watch registered a frantic text from his wife, who had woken up to a flashing alert about him from NGC Medical Center. He shot back a smiley face to reassure her and braced himself for a longer conversation later.

This isn't science fiction

This scenario may sound futuristic, but many aspects of it are here already. Even if the healthcare industry doesn't yet offer these capabilities, similar ones are available in other industries. Take banking, for example. Many of the technologies and business processes in banking are like those that Tony benefitted from in our example.

Banks have already seen their future. While there are still bank branches and headquarters buildings for specialized transactions, the core of the banking experience for many customers is already the bank website, the mobile app, and the chatbot. They keep track of transactions and identify potentially fraudulent ones, dispense financial advice through "robo-advisors," send real-time alerts about fraud or low balances, and allow the customer to go about their financial business with convenience and flexibility. We can wire money from our own bank to one in Abu Dhabi in a few minutes—at low cost and with little risk of fraud. Some countries, such as the U.K., have instituted "open banking" systems that let customers aggregate all their assets and transactions across banks in one place.

Healthcare isn't at that point yet, but it will be over the next decade or so. Moving money and financial transaction information is less complex than moving health information, but the healthcare industry will need to figure out the equivalent of what banks have already figured out: how to coordinate different currencies and financial instruments across institutions. We have the rudiments now. Healthcare systems around the world all generally use the same disease classification (ICD-11), though each country has local variations. Providers are beginning to share data with other healthcare institutions, especially those who have the same EHR systems. EHR data is increasingly downloadable into personal devices. We have a long way to go before we achieve the kind of transparency Tony's world will need, but both technology and industry forces are aligning to push things in the right direction.

We expect that the core of the patient's medical experience will shift toward online portals, mobile apps, wearable devices, and AI-based recommendations. Physicians and other care providers will make their diagnoses and treatment recommendations with the aid of machine learning models. Many drugs will be designed, developed, and tested with the aid of AI algorithms. Hospitals, clinics, and physicians' offices will still be necessary for medical procedures, but they can be increasingly decentralized and mobile, like the MMF that pulled into Tony's driveway.

Healthcare providers will gather and analyze data from a wide variety of medical devices and sensors, both in the home and from wearables on (and in) patients' bodies. As it did for Tony, AI will make sense of all the data, make ongoing healthcare recommendations, and let the patient know when he or she needs to be seen by a clinician. AI will drive precision medicine, in which every drug and treatment approach is tailored to a patient's genome, proteome, biome, and living/social/economic situation.

Care will increasingly be decentralized, delivered in drug and grocery stores or via mobile, highly connected care facilities like the one that made Tony's high-tech house call. Provider institutions will need to integrate and analyze all the data streaming from, to, and about the patient. Care will be data-driven, continuous, predictive, and prescriptive. Just as a bank tells you that you are unlikely to outlive your retirement investments, a healthcare provider will tell you that your New Year's Eve behaviors are likely to shorten your lifespan.

The signs of this transition are too numerous to doubt. Watches today can track heart rates, blood oxygen, and falls. Home devices already monitor body weight, blood oxygen, blood glucose, fetal heartbeats, medication adherence, and many other conditions. Clinics are proliferating in drug and grocery stores, and mobile clinics and "health vans" are growing in popularity. AI-based diagnosis and treatment innovations are described daily in medical and technology journals.

These capabilities are beginning to create new partnerships. As with Tony's "Northwestern Google Cigna" care provider, hospitals can't accomplish this data integration alone. Companies that are heavily focused on data capture, storage, and analysis have already signaled their interest in managing patient data. Google, Microsoft, Amazon, and Facebook have made forays into healthcare, some successful and some not. Even the companies with failed initiatives, however—Microsoft's HealthVault, for example—continue to pursue healthcare capabilities. In 2020 Microsoft paid $16 billion to acquire Nuance, a leading provider of healthcare natural language processing software.

Payers and providers, often at odds over whether care is necessary and how much it should cost, are beginning to collaborate more. We expect that they will partner and perhaps combine, as some have already. If incentives are aligned correctly, both parties will have an interest in keeping patients well, in providing effective but low-cost care, and making data-driven decisions. They need to share data to see the entire picture of a patient's health. And both sides can benefit from relationships with tech companies that have mastered data capture, analysis, and presentation.

If traditional healthcare providers are to survive, they will need to play an important role in this digital and intelligent future. Their services overall are enormously expensive, and becoming more so all the time. Electronic medical record systems may already be pervasive in providers across many countries, but most are only good at record-keeping and can't make data-driven recommendations or flag impending problems. Individual providers don't share their data with other providers, don't gather data from wearables or home devices, and don't even attempt to have a holistic view of patients' health. They will need to get smarter, more efficient, and more digital, or get out of the business.

What's in this book?

There is no shortage of books about AI, or even AI in healthcare, but this book is especially for healthcare provider executives. They are open to the possibilities that AI might transform healthcare, but most are not interested in being on the bleeding edge of AI research. They want to make smart decisions about investing in, implementing, and managing AI systems over the next several years.

The authors represent several points of view. Tom Davenport is an expert in the application of AI within large organizations, and has done considerable research and consulting with healthcare providers. John Glaser has been a senior executive of a leading healthcare provider, and then a senior executive in several healthcare IT firms. Elizabeth Gardner has covered health information technology for decades as a journalist with several leading publications in the field. We all have a strong interest in helping healthcare executives, managers, and practitioners make better use of emerging technologies, and we all agree that AI is potentially transformative.

We're not yet dazzled by the technology. We know that it's still early days for AI, and that there is more action in the research lab than at the hospital bedside. However, we're confident that understanding and thinking clearly about AI's place in a medical institution now will help lay the groundwork for effective adoption at the right time. We hope we are clear about what's ready for production deployment today, and what won't be fully cooked for at least a few more years.

Here is a quick guide to the chapters, so that readers can rapidly turn to those that are most interesting and relevant:

Chapter 1: Introduction to Artificial Intelligence in Healthcare

This introductory chapter describes the overall context for AI in healthcare, why its time has come (or is rapidly coming), and the factors that will govern its growth.

Chapter 2: AI Technologies and Their Impact on Strategy

We discuss the major types of AI, along with their impacts on business models and value-based care and the factors that govern organizational adoption.

Chapter 3: AI for Diagnosis and Treatment

We review this most tantalizing set of healthcare use cases for AI—some that are only in the lab and some now in clinical practice.

Chapter 4: AI-Based Drugs, Devices, Facilities, and the Like

AI is increasingly being used to develop new drugs, analyze data from medical devices, and even to monitor and capture clinician/patient interactions in examination rooms.

Chapter 5: AI for Engaging Patients and Improving Health

AI is being employed for helping patients manage their own health in terms of dealing with chronic disease, changing patient behavior, and maintaining wellness.

Chapter 6: Administering and Paying for Healthcare With AI

Some of the most financially valuable and easiest-to-implement AI applications are those involved in revenue cycle, administrative operations, and procurement and supply chain management.

Chapter 7: The Impacts of AI On Human Healthcare Providers

AI has yet to put doctors or nurses out of work, and it is unlikely to do so anytime soon. But it will have substantial impacts on their jobs, and organizations should prepare for them now.

Chapter 8: Recognizing and Managing AI-Associated Risks

This chapter describes the challenges and risks that AI must overcome before it can have a major impact on healthcare, including regulatory approval, algorithmic concerns, privacy issues, and legal liability.

Chapter 9: Moving Forward: How to Integrate AI Into Your Organization

The final chapter addresses the ways in which healthcare providers can strategize, organize, and architect for AI.

While the book is organized into chapters that reflect groups of related topics and uses of AI, discussion of some topics occurs across several chapters.

Management of AI

Chapter 9 is devoted to this topic. However, aspects of management are also discussed in other chapters:

- Chapter 1 outlines some actions management can take to accelerate AI adoption in their organization
- Chapter 2 examines organizational factors that impact the ability of healthcare organizations to implement new AI-enabled business models
- Chapter 3 discusses examples of AI centers of excellence
- Chapter 7 examines the impact of AI on the provider workforce and approaches to manage that impact
- Chapter 8 discusses AI risks and steps that can be taken to manage those risks.

Regulation of AI

When AI directly affects how care is delivered, augmenting the capabilities of medical devices and helping create new medications, it will invite regulatory oversight. We discuss this topic at some length in Chapter 8. In addition:

- Chapter 3 touches on the regulation of AI-driven clinician decision aids

- Chapter 4 touches upon AI regulation of new therapeutic compounds and devices
- Chapter 5 reviews regulation of devices used by consumers to manage their health.

Pace of AI adoption

The pace and form of AI adoption in healthcare will be governed by several factors. These factors are explored in several chapters.

- Chapter 1 reviews some characteristics of the healthcare industry that impact adoption
- Chapter 2 examines factors that inhibit or ease the adoption of new business models by healthcare organizations
- Chapter 5 explores issues facing consumer adoption of AI-based healthcare apps
- Chapter 8 examines AI risk factors that must be mitigated for broad AI adoption to occur
- Chapter 9 outlines management steps to be taken to help ensure the successful implementation of a portfolio of AI applications.

1

Introduction to artificial intelligence in healthcare

1.1   Introduction

Starting with the earliest days of what we now call information technology, each decade has brought us a new and transformative development. The 1960s saw the mainframe computer shrink from its original room-sized form into a manageable tool for big business to use for heavy-duty number-crunching. The 1970s produced the minicomputer, giving that same access to smaller businesses and organizations (including hospitals, many of which started their digital journey with a DEC or Data General minicomputer). In the 1980s the networked personal computer arrived, bringing information technology to even the tiniest businesses, and for the first time into the home. The 1990s brought the Internet out of its shadowy government/academic world and into commercial use. The 2000s introduced cellphones small enough to fit in a pocket, and by the end of the decade, smartphones. It's a little too soon at this writing to be certain what the 2010s will be remembered for, but big data and the Internet of Things are contenders.

The cumulative impact of these technologies would stupefy a time-traveler from the 1950s. What would stupefy us if we could jump forward 70 years? What will be the IT hallmark of the 2020s?

Artificial intelligence, of course. AI has been brewing for a long time—since the 1950s in fact—but this is its decade to start making noticeable inroads into everyday life. Alexa may already live on your kitchen counter, responding to oral requests to dim the lights, close the garage door, look up recipes, and find music suitable for cooking to. Maybe your car stops automatically before you hit the car in front of you and tells you

1

how to avoid the slowdown from the accident up ahead (involving cars not as smart as yours). Maybe your browser senses your yearning to travel and tries to lure you out with bargain fares to Mexico and ads for highly rated luggage.

AI's potential to eventually dwarf all previous IT advances and transform our lives in fundamental, unpredictable ways is beyond the scope of this book. But its potential to transform every aspect of medicine and healthcare is here, now. It's vital for healthcare industry leaders, embarking on this AI journey, to understand, as best we can, how to reap its benefits. We must avoid, on the one hand, the lure of snake oil and, on the other, the possible dangers of employing a set of technologies whose capabilities and vulnerabilities even its makers don't fully understand.

AI may already be built into your building controls, medical devices, billing systems, and electronic health records. As these capabilities evolve, AI will transform the healthcare field in ways that no one can truly anticipate or plan for. But we will help you try.

1.2   Definition of artificial intelligence

"Artificial intelligence" is as difficult to define as "intelligence." One definition often used is "computer systems that perceive their environment in some manner and respond with actions to maximize their chance of success – activities generally associated with intelligent beings" (Poole 1998, 1). "Success" can be parking within the lines, appropriately identifying impending equipment failure, or correctly interpreting a radiology image.

The term AI covers an expansive range of capabilities: predicting the future with machine learning; voice recognition; contextually aware interactions ("people like you bought these products"); pattern identification (modeling traffic-light sequences to minimize rush-hour slowdowns); or complex process automation (extracting information across multiple systems and documents to create an accurate bill).

A comprehensive review of potential healthcare AI applications would be (a) many times longer than we have space to describe or you have time to read and (b) outdated before we finished typing the last sentence. However, we will review a diverse set of applications for AI in this book to help you understand its current state and potential. Just a few areas that we'll touch on in later chapters include:

Diagnosis and treatment

- Detection of neurological problems by examining facial micro-expressions
- Image interpretation in radiology and pathology
- Mining genomic data to identify Covid disease severity risk
- Adapting the interface of the electronic health record to help clinicians focus on relevant patient information.

Medications and devices

- Accelerating drug development using AI-based compound design
- Tailoring treatment plans for diseases such as prostate cancer
- Analysis of heart rhythm anomalies using wearable devices
- Smart exam rooms that generate care documentation based on the image and voice analysis of the patient–provider interaction.

Disease management and patient engagement

- Examination of the health of the digestive tract through analysis of images captured by a smart pill
- Artificial pancreas based on AI algorithms
- AI-guided management of chronic kidney disease
- Digital therapy support for patients with depression and anxiety.

Administrative uses

- Natural language processing to analyze a physician's documentation and generate accurate billing codes
- Automated prior authorization through analysis of a patient's medical record
- Identification of patterns of insurance fraud
- Optimization of operating room utilization.

1.3   Why now?

Only now is AI starting to play a noticeable role in healthcare and daily life. Why? Because we finally have an "ecosystem" that can support it.

All new technologies need an ecosystem to give them traction. Cars needed roads, gas stations, traffic laws, and people who wanted to go places. Mobile devices needed small but powerful chips that don't overheat, as well as high-speed wireless networks, location awareness, long-lasting rechargeable batteries, and an abundance of easily accessible apps.

AI needed and now has:

Processing power. Computers keep getting more powerful and efficient, and programming techniques like deep learning are enabling them to handle information the way brains do. Graphics processing units (GPUs) that once powered video games now make possible complex image recognition. Millions of computers can work together to tackle the most complex computations. Cloud services allow any individual or enterprise to tap extraordinary amounts of storage and processing capability on demand.

Environment-awareness technologies. Highly miniaturized and specialized sensors and the "Internet of Things" can generate data for, and execute instructions from, AI-enabled systems. Advances in packaging can place them almost anywhere, from outer space to inside the body.

Staggering amounts of diverse data. From the human genome to web browser cookies to cellphone traffic to CT and MRI scans, we have more information than we can understand unaided. We currently generate 2.5 quintillion bytes per day—and that number is not going to stop growing.

A digital foundation. As we will discuss later in this book, AI is usually part of something else: a product or a service. AI can improve the safety of a car by detecting lane drift, or suggest diagnoses to a physician as they enter a patient's orders into an electronic health record (EHR) system. AI as a standalone application has always struggled since it is outside of the workflow and its use requires extra steps. With the broad adoption of a digital foundation (e.g., population health applications, electronic health records, and mobile device apps), AI is much easier to use and therefore accept.

Maturity of business models. Across all industries, organizations are beginning to understand how to leverage AI to improve their offerings and make them more competitive. AI adds value in all kinds of ways, from equipment that alerts users when it's about to break down to personal assistant bots that recommend a nice restaurant and the perfect gift for your spouse's upcoming birthday. Many of these business models also can be applied to healthcare.

1.4   The AI market

AI applications could save the U.S. healthcare system $150 billion a year by 2026, according to a 2020 analysis by the consulting firm Accenture (Collier 2020). The areas they identify with the most growth potential include robotic-assisted surgery, virtual nursing assistants, and administrative workflow assistance.

This value potential—not unique to healthcare—has resulted in the explosive growth in the market for AI software, hardware, and services. In 2019, the global artificial intelligence market was estimated to be US$27 billion. The market is expected to grow at a compound annual growth rate of 33 percent, reaching US$267 billion by 2027 (Fortune Business Insights 2021).

Artificial intelligence has become more than a fast-growing market. It has also become a form of technology arms race between countries; in particular between the world's two superpowers China and the U.S.A. These countries see the importance of establishing a dominant and vibrant AI technology position for their economies and the defense of their country.

In 1990, fewer than 1,000 AI scientific papers were published in China. In 2015, that number had become 39,000 papers. In 1990, 7,000 AI scientific papers were published in the U.S.A. In 2015, that number had become 25,000 papers (Li 2021). These data highlight the significant increase in public and private sector AI research investment and output. Most noteworthy is the increased emphasis on AI by China—including some massive systems for AI-enabled telemedicine.

Healthcare investors have been swept up in the global excitement in artificial intelligence. They see the market opportunities that result from the adoption of the example uses cited above. As can be seen in Table 1.1, the level of investment and the number of deals led by U.S. venture and private equity firms has increased significantly since 2015 (CB Insights 2020).

The significant research and investment interest in artificial intelligence will result in major advances in the capabilities, accessibility, and price/performance of AI-based products and services. Like the Internet and mobile devices, AI is poised to grow by leaps and begin to transform entire industries.

These leaps have already begun. For example, the ImageNet Large Scale Visual Recognition Challenge, held annually since 2010 under the auspices of Princeton University and the Stanford University Vision Lab, evaluates algorithms for object detection and image classification at large scale. In the 2011 challenge, the error rate was 26 percent. By 2016, the error rate was 3 percent. The best performing human has an error rate of 5 percent (Howell 2019).

Table 1.1   Level of investment and number of deals in AI in the U.S.A.

Year	Deals	Total funding amount ($M)
2020 (through Q3)	289	4,500
2019	386	4,100
2018	306	3,200
2017	244	1,800
2016	172	1,200
2015	121	500

Source: CB Insights 2020.

1.5   Hype and hope

Every transformative technology goes through a chaotic and confusing period as it evolves. What does healthcare leadership need to understand about AI to make informed decisions?

Some may recall similar discussions in the late 1990s regarding the Internet. What is this new technology? What benefits and risks does it carry for our organization? How about this "website" that the marketing department wants funding for? A quarter-century later, the Internet has permeated every facet of every organization's business, bringing benefits and risks that no C-suite could have begun to comprehend the day it first heard the word "Internet."

The research and consulting firm Gartner, Inc., has developed a "Hype Cycle" framework that describes how a technology matures: how its capabilities evolve and how organizations come to understand its value.

Any technology's life cycle has five phases (Gartner 2021a):

- *Innovation Trigger:* A potential technology breakthrough kicks things off. Early proof-of-concept stories and media interest trigger significant publicity. Often no usable products exist, and commercial viability is unproven.
- *Peak of Inflated Expectations:* Early publicity produces a number of success stories—often accompanied by scores of failures. Some companies take action; many do not.
- *Trough of Disillusionment:* Interest wanes as experiments and implementations fail to deliver. Producers of the technology shake out or fail. Investments continue only if the surviving providers improve their products to the satisfaction of early adopters.
- *Slope of Enlightenment:* More instances of how the technology can benefit the enterprise start to crystallize and become more widely understood. Second- and third-generation products appear from technology providers. More enterprises fund pilots; conservative companies remain cautious.
- *Plateau of Productivity:* Mainstream adoption starts to take off. Criteria for assessing provider viability are more clearly defined. The technology's broad market applicability and relevance are clearly paying off.

There comes a point in the development of every technology when its value, or lack of value, starts to become clear. Sometimes an organization decides to adopt a technology before that point, hoping to gain a competitive edge or solve a specific problem. Some technologies obviously fail before an organization decides to invest in them. For others, it becomes clear in hindsight that the organization should have invested sooner.

Take smartphones and tablets, for example. In healthcare, they posed a significant challenge to data management, patient privacy, and security as soon as individual clinicians and employees started using them in the work environment. They may initially have attracted the IT department's attention as a problem rather than an opportunity. Now, of course, hospitals and other healthcare organizations are purchasing these devices as a part of their overall information system infrastructure and embracing those challenges to get the benefits of usability and easy data sharing that smartphones and tablets enable.

At what point should healthcare executives have known that smart-phones and tablets were here to stay and were something to be leveraged and managed? Did their early adopters have an advantage in the market? Would there have been a disadvantage in getting in early?

These questions can be asked now about AI. It is difficult to understand the potential maturity of a technology when the discussion is cloaked in a fog of either unwarranted exuberance or overwhelming skepticism. This difficulty is compounded because AI is not a single technology but several, encompassing diverse capabilities and applications.

When the Gartner Hype Cycle is applied to AI, it's clear that many of the AI technologies are still headed toward the peak of inflated expectations, while others are entering the trough of disillusionment. Almost no AI technologies have arrived at the stages of the slope of enlightenment and the plateau of productivity (Gartner 2021b).

Healthcare organizations may understandably hesitate to invest at scale in technologies that are at the peak of inflated expectations. It's perfectly reasonable to let the market evolve and the products mature before you commit. On the other hand, you may decide that the technology has significant potential if it works even slightly as promised, and that it's time to conduct pilots to begin to understand that potential and how to use it. If it can help you predict which ICU patients are likely to "crash" in the next 72 hours, or which segments of your population are most at risk of developing diabetes in the next two years, it might be worth the investment.

Considering technologies in the context of the Hype Cycle isn't just about avoiding risk: it's about analyzing the potential rewards and determining the circumstances under which the organization is willing to brave the trough of disillusionment and have a chance of reaping those rewards. These analyses will be different for every organization and for every technology.

1.6 From bench to bedside: factors affecting the pace of implementation

Though many healthcare providers can start taking advantage of AI now for administration, billing, maintenance, and other applications that don't directly touch patients, we expect it will be ten years or more before AI starts to exert a truly transformative effect on healthcare delivery. Given the rapid pace of invention and innovation, and the enormous investment we discussed above, why can't we have clinical transformation sooner? What factors will determine how quickly healthcare moves from the left side of the Hype Cycle (headed toward peak expectations and disillusionment) to the right side (headed toward enlightenment and productivity)?

We discuss some of the reasons elsewhere in this book. The regulatory approval process will slow things down. The natural caution associated with the Hype Cycle described above is another factor. Yet another is the narrow use case, where an AI application can do a single task as well as, or better than, a human clinician, but can't handle the dozen other tasks that make up the human clinician's daily routine. Here are some other factors.

1.6.1 Data integration

Data is the fuel of AI. Despite some progress over the past couple of decades, healthcare data is generally still as fragmented and siloed as the healthcare system that creates it, at least in the U.S.A. Most hospitals and group medical practices have their own EHR data and little else. Payers generally have only claims data, although some are partnering with providers to get access to their EHR data. It is extremely rare to have all a patient's healthcare data—across all providers and payers—available in one easily accessible repository.

Some national healthcare systems have a common EHR system, which makes it relatively straightforward to both gather data to train models and to integrate new AI-based scoring systems into clinical practice. For example, the U.K.'s NHS, which doesn't have an overall common EHR system but does have one for general practitioners, has created and deployed an "Electronic Frailty Index" from EHR data. The machine learning model creates a score for elderly patients that is integrated within the EHR system. If the GP sees a patient with a severe or moderate frailty index, special care measures (such as a medication review or falls risk assessment) are mandated or recommended (Clegg 2016).

Limited data integration does not impact all clinical AI algorithms. AI methods directed to interpreting radiology images do not require the integration of a broad range of EHR data. However, exciting AI opportunities, such as comparative effectiveness determination and understanding the factors that increase the risk of disease, will be hobbled by poor interoperability. Moreover, as the range of health-related data increases to include, for example, social determinants of health and wearable sensors, limited data integration will become increasingly problematic.

AI requires, and may drive, better data integration and cooperation.

1.6.2   Clinician education and workflow

Clinicians will need substantial education in AI to use it effectively in clinical practice. Medical schools have yet to integrate AI across the curriculum (and only a few have addressed digital or information technologies of any type, or personalized/precision medical care, in formal courses).

Clinicians may resist using AI systems that don't fit well into clinical workflows. This complaint has been leveled against EHRs in general, but they are so critical to modern medical practice that most physicians use them anyway. If AI systems require separate systems, apps, APIs, or logins, they are much less likely to be adopted. AI will need to be integrated into EHRs to be widely deployed with any success.

1.6.3   Ethical considerations

Ethical AI is a concern for all industries but a greater one for healthcare. As a social good, healthcare confronts ethical issues such as right to life, assisted suicide, patient rights in clinical research, and the allocation of scare healthcare resources.

The following ethical principles were developed by the World Health Organization in 2021 for AI use in healthcare:

Protecting human autonomy. In the context of healthcare, this means that humans should remain in control of healthcare systems and medical decisions; privacy and confidentiality should be protected; and patients must give valid informed consent through appropriate legal frameworks for data protection.

Promoting human well-being and safety and the public interest. The designers of AI technologies should satisfy regulatory requirements for safety, accuracy, and efficacy for well-defined use cases or indications. Measures of quality control in practice and quality improvement in the use of AI must be available.

Ensuring transparency, explainability, and intelligibility. Transparency requires that sufficient information be published or documented before the design or deployment of an AI technology. Such information must be easily accessible and facilitate meaningful public consultation and debate on how the technology is designed and how it should or should not be used.

Fostering responsibility and accountability. Although AI technologies perform specific tasks, it is the responsibility of stakeholders to ensure that they are used under appropriate conditions and by appropriately trained people. Effective mechanisms should be available for questioning and for redress for individuals and groups that are adversely affected by decisions based on algorithms.

Ensuring inclusiveness and equity. Inclusiveness requires that AI for health be designed to encourage the widest possible equitable use and access, irrespective of age, sex, gender, income, race, ethnicity, sexual orientation, ability, or other characteristics protected under human rights codes.

Promoting AI that is responsive and sustainable. Designers, developers, and users should continuously and transparently assess AI applications during actual use to determine whether AI responds adequately and appropriately to expectations and requirements. AI systems should also be designed to minimize their environmental consequences and increase energy efficiency. Governments and companies should address anticipated disruptions in the workplace, including training for healthcare workers to adapt to the use of AI systems, and potential job losses due to use of automated systems. (World Health Organization 2021)

Complying with all of these principles, however reasonable they seem, will not be easy or even possible for many AI systems. We expect that close adherence to them will slow down their development and adoption.

1.6.4   The scientific basis of medical care

Healthcare is different from most industries in the extent to which it must rely on public scientific methods to introduce new products and practices. As patients, we appreciate the conservative approach to new treatments. Studies to determine the clinical utility of incorporating AI into clinical practice will take years: to conduct each study, to publish the results, for the medical community to accept the results and alter clinical practice, and for the payers to approve reimbursement. The development and introduction of most consumer-based AI products and services, such as driving assistance, do not undergo this degree of public scientific rigor.

1.6.5   Reimbursement

Healthcare providers around the world must worry about how to pay for any innovation in healthcare. In the best case, innovations pay for themselves, allowing providers to offer better care at the same cost, or to offer the same quality care at lower cost. (Whether they actually do reduce the cost is a topic beyond the scope of this book.)

Some AI-based innovations may fit this best-case scenario, but many will require payer approval for providers to afford to adopt them. In the U.K., the National Health Service announced in 2019 that it would begin to reimburse for AI-based care in 2020 to incentivize more rapid adoption, though details have been sketchy (Mari 2019). The NHS is also investing about £140 million in AI for healthcare through the NHS AI Lab (NHS AI Lab 2021).

In China, in part because of the Covid-19 pandemic, the Chinese National Health Commission approved reimbursement for online consultations using AI and other digital tools in 2020. China has seen massive growth in the use of AI for general practitioner advice, which can determine whether a face-to-face consultation is required. We could find no evidence that some of the more advanced image detection use cases are reimbursed (or in clinical practice) in China, although there are plenty of startups in that space.

At this writing, only a few AI-based applications—including one for diagnosing blood clots in the brain and another for diabetic retinopathy—have been approved for reimbursement by the U.S. Centers for Medicare and Medicaid Services (CMS), which pays for about half of U.S. healthcare. It is expected that private insurers will follow the lead of CMS, but they haven't done so publicly yet.

We believe that in the U.S.A., the tipping point of adoption will depend on the speed with which healthcare moves to value-based payment models, which require providers to support their patients' *health* rather than simply providing health *care* for particular illnesses or medical issues. It's impossible to overstate how dramatically the average healthcare organization would have to change, at every level, if all its revenue became value-based—one reason that this new model will take time to become the broad foundation of healthcare. Organizations will need to understand and manage their patient populations in new ways, and AI-enabled analytics may be their best route to doing so.

1.6.6   Planning for adoption

The advantage of a deliberate pace for AI adoption? It gives healthcare organizations time to plan and adapt. Positioning your organization for success depends on several factors:

- AI adoption will move faster in organizations that declare adoption to be a strategic priority than in organizations that view it as a novelty or niche technology.

- Organizations that have deployed core transaction applications, such as electronic health records and revenue cycle applications, will be better positioned to incorporate AI into the workflow.
- This transformation will be simpler and faster in organizations that have a base of applications from one vendor across the enterprise than those with applications from multiple vendors.
- Organizations will adopt AI more quickly and smoothly if they already know how to move new technologies from pilot to broad deployment and manage the accompanying workflow and/or cultural changes.

Healthcare organizations may decide to focus on administrative applications as clinical use evolves. Administrative adoption does not face the same challenges confronting clinical use. Administrative applications often pay for themselves and do not rely on payer reimbursement. These applications are not regulated since they do not directly impact clinical care. Administrative applications are not addressed by the same scientific process as new medical interventions.

In this chapter we defined artificial intelligence and examined advances that have brought AI to center stage. We reviewed the AI product and service market and noted that AI is in the early stages of technology maturity. We discussed factors that will affect the pace of AI adoption and explored factors that will enable organizations to increase the speed of AI adoption.

In the next chapter, we will discuss AI technologies and explore the potential impact of AI on healthcare organization business models.

References

CB Insights (2020). Healthcare AI trends to watch, November 12. https://www.cbinsights.com/research/report/ai-trends-healthcare/.

Clegg, A., Bates, C., Young, J., et al. (2016). Development and validation of an electronic frailty index using routine primary care electronic health record data. *Age and Ageing*, 45(3): 353–60. https://doi.org/10.1093/ageing/afw039 [published correction appears in *Age and Ageing*, January 17, 2017].

Collier, M. (2020). Artificial intelligence: healthcare's new nervous system. *Accenture*, July 30. http://www.accenture.com/au-en/insights/health/artificial-intelligence-healthcare.

Fortune Business Insights (2021). Artificial intelligence market to reach USD 266.92 billion by 2027. Press release, May 7.

Gartner (2021a). Gartner Hype Cycle. https://www.gartner.com/en/research/methodologies/gartner-hype-cycle.

Gartner (2021b). Gartner identifies four trends driving near-term artificial intelligence innovation. https://www.gartner.com/en/newsroom/press-releases/2021-09-07-gartner-identifies-four-trends-driving-near-term-artificial-intelligence-innovation.

Howell, M. and Stevens, J.P. (2019). *Understanding Healthcare Delivery Science.* New York: McGraw-Hill.

Li, D., Tong, T. and Xiao, Y. (2021). Is China emerging as the global leader in AI? *Harvard Business Review,* February 18.

Mari, A. (2019). NHS to provide funds to reward use of AI in health service. *Computer Weekly,* June 6.

NHS AI Lab. (2021). https://www.nhsx.nhs.uk/ai-lab/ (accessed December 7, 2021).

Poole, D., Mackworth, A. and Goebel, R. (1998). *Computational Intelligence: A Logical Approach.* New York: Oxford University Press.

World Health Organization (2021). Ethics and governance of artificial intelligence for health: WHO guidance. World Health Organization.

2   AI technologies and their impact on strategy

2.1   Introduction

The cluster of technologies that make up today's artificial intelligence will transform industries and companies in diverse and probably unpredictable ways. As previously noted, they've already infiltrated multiple aspects of healthcare. Today's leaders have a choice: they can study how these technologies will transform their industry and try to build that transformation into their strategic planning or they can watch their competitors do it and try to catch up later.

2.2   Types of AI technologies

AI is an umbrella term encompassing a variety of approaches (Davenport 2019). Since different AI technologies support different AI applications and "use cases," it's important for leaders of organizations to know what technologies and related capabilities they are investing in.

2.2.1   Machine learning: neural networks and deep learning

Machine learning is a statistical technique for fitting models to data and predicting future outcomes based on past ones. In machine learning, the algorithm is trained from the data. For example, the computer "reads" many images of cars (that have to be labeled as cars) and devises its own statistical algorithm for predicting that an unlabeled image is a car.

Machine learning is one of the most common forms of AI, with many potential applications. In a 2018 Deloitte survey of 1,100 U.S. managers whose organizations were already pursuing AI, 63 percent of companies surveyed were employing machine learning in their businesses (Deloitte Insights 2018). Example AI applications are using predictive maintenance to reduce equipment downtime and optimize advertising buying and placement.

In healthcare, the most common application of traditional machine learning is precision medicine: predicting what treatment protocols are likely to succeed with a given patient based on their attributes and the treatment context (Lee 2018). Most machine learning and precision medicine applications use "supervised learning," which requires a training dataset for which the outcome variable is known (e.g., onset of disease or presence of a tumor).

A more complex form of machine learning is the neural network (Sordo 2002), used for categorization applications such as determining whether a patient will develop a particular disease. It views problems in terms of inputs, outputs, and the weights of variables or "features" that associate inputs with outputs.

The most complex forms of machine learning involve "deep learning": neural network models with many levels of features or variables that predict outcomes. Deep learning algorithms are well suited to image recognition and can learn to recognize potentially cancerous lesions in radiology images (Fakoor 2013). Deep learning is increasingly being applied to radiomics, or the detection of clinically relevant features in imaging data beyond what can be perceived by the human eye (Vial 2018). Deep learning, when applied to oncology-oriented image analysis, appears to promise greater accuracy in diagnosis than an earlier generation of automated tools for image analysis, known as computer-aided detection or CAD.

Deep learning can identify more complex and intricate patterns than machine learning and is more computationally efficient. However, the deep learning model may be more difficult to explain to a human since the algorithm does not use human criteria to determine which features of an image are relevant. Instead, for example, it focuses on the brightness of pixels in an image and their relationship to each other.

Deep learning is also increasingly used for speech recognition and, as such, is a form of natural language processing (NLP), described below.

2.2.2   Natural language processing

Natural language processing, or teaching computers to make sense of human language, has been a goal of AI researchers since the 1950s. NLP includes applications such as speech recognition, text analysis, and translation. There are two basic approaches: statistical and semantic. Statistical NLP is based on machine learning (deep learning neural networks in particular) and has contributed to a recent increase in accuracy of recognition. Statistical NLP uses statistics to figure out the most likely word or phrase spoken or in text, given its context. For example, determining whether the word is "patients" or "patience" depends on how often that word appears in the context of a radiology report.

Semantic NLP breaks a body of text or spoken word into its components—sentences, subject, verb, object, etc.—and proceeds to interpret from there. For example, in the sentence "heat the water" it can decide that the word heat is a verb in the sentence rather than a noun.

In healthcare, the dominant applications of NLP involve the creation, understanding, and classification of clinical documentation and published research. NLP systems can analyze unstructured clinical notes on patients, prepare reports (e.g., on radiology examinations), transcribe patient interactions and conduct conversational AI. NLP is perhaps the most widely applied AI technology in healthcare. Just one vendor, Nuance (now owned by Microsoft), claims to have more than 55 percent of physicians and 75 percent of radiologists in the U.S.A. as customers, and is used in 77 percent of U.S. hospitals (Morse 2021).

2.2.3   Rule-based expert systems

"Expert systems" based on collections of "if–then" rules were the dominant technology for AI in the 1980s. In healthcare, they were (and still are) widely employed for clinical decision support (Davenport 2018), particularly in electronic health records. A certain diagnosis triggers reminders to order tests or schedule follow-up appointments. A prescription triggers a drug interaction warning.

Expert systems require human experts and knowledge engineers to construct rules. Such systems work well up to a point and are easy to understand (although clinicians must trust the experts who have made the rules). However, when the rules start to number in the thousands, they can conflict with each other and the systems break down or, worse, become unpredictable. Updating the rules quickly enough to keep with new knowledge is increasingly impossible. Expert systems are slowly being replaced in healthcare by machine learning algorithms that provide more precise recommendations and can update themselves if trained on new data.

2.2.4   Physical robots

More than 200,000 industrial robots are installed each year around the world. They perform pre-defined tasks: lifting, repositioning, welding, or assembling objects. They deliver supplies in hospitals. Surgical robots, approved in the U.S.A. in 2000, aren't AI: they provide "superpowers" to surgeons, improving their vision and precision in head and neck surgery, prostate resections, and gynecological procedures (Hussain 2014), but the surgeon still makes the decisions. The combination of these capabilities with the power of true AI may someday make robots into true collaborators, rather than just tools. There are autonomous and semi-autonomous surgical robots in research labs, but not yet in operating rooms (Metz 2021).

2.2.5   Robotic process automation

Robotic process automation (RPA) doesn't involve physical robots, just software. It relies on a combination of workflow, business rules and "presentation layer" integration with information systems to act like a semi-intelligent user of the systems. It can perform structured digital tasks for administrative and clinical operations as if it were a human user following a script or rules. Compared with other forms of AI, RPAs are inexpensive, easy to program, and transparent in their actions.

In healthcare, RPA can handle repetitive tasks like requesting prior authorization, ensuring that the steps a patient needs to take to prepare for surgery are followed, updating patient records, or ensuring that a claim is complete before submitting it for payment. When combined with other technologies like image recognition, it can be used to extract data from document images and put it into transactional systems (Bush 2018). Some call the combination of RPA and machine learning "intelligent process automation."

2.2.6   AI vs. human intelligence

We've described these diverse technologies individually, but increasingly they are being combined and integrated: robots are getting AI-based "brains" and image recognition is being integrated with RPA. Eventually composite solutions will become the norm.

Where can AI help humans perform better, and which sources of tedium can it take over entirely so that humans can use their (still) superior abilities and limited time most effectively? Leaders will find themselves asking that question over and over as AI becomes more sophisticated and capable of a broader range of tasks.

Complex decisions. Trained, skilled, and experienced people remain terrific at recognizing patterns, making decisions, handling emotional situations, and managing complex processes. They can assess the ethics of a situation with a subtlety that an AI algorithm cannot. Humans can make complex "value" decisions that are difficult for AI. (For example, should a patient dying of Covid be allowed to see her children, even if it raises their risk of infection? AI can "run the numbers" but can't weigh the feelings of the mother and the children.)

Underlying rules. Deep learning and other AI techniques run into performance limitations when we can't explain the underlying rules—either because we don't yet understand them or because they defy explanation. Why is sleep necessary? Why do some people get cancer while others do not? We don't (yet) know the rules that would answer these questions and hence our data is unlikely to have captured the variables necessary to suggest applicable rules. Deep learning and machine learning can identify the set of data that is correlated with a particular outcome, such as the presence or absence of a tumor. By design these algorithms don't identify causality and hence don't identify rules, whether hidden or obvious, although the correlations they draw can point the way to possible rules.

Sometimes humans understand "hidden" rules but would not be able to explain them to an algorithm, particularly in cases where we are relying on instincts or bursts of creative insight.

Continuous vs. discrete variables. At times, deep learning techniques perform poorly on predicting continuous (rather than discrete) variables. Traditional regression analyses are better equipped to predict continuous variables, such as IQ. Discrete variables enable a piece of data to be classified. Eye color can be classified as blue, brown, hazel, etc.

Machine learning needs to classify variables: for example, to determine whether a data class helps to identify an object in an image. While continuous data can often be converted into data classes—for example, a range of temperature could be divided into lukewarm, warm, and hot—that classification can, in some cases, make the data less effective as a predictor variable.

Decision trees and regressions. Basic if–then–else decision trees remain very efficient ways to provide structure to a decision process and ensure that all possibilities have been weighed.

In fact, once an AI algorithm has been developed and the classification scoring system developed, the algorithm is sometimes converted to a decision tree to improve run time computer performance and improve explainability. Decision trees convey a sequence of logic: if this, then do X and proceed to the next step. Machine learning algorithms do not create a sequence of logical steps to arrive at a conclusion. Decision trees don't require the same amount of computation effort to process as a machine learning algorithm and it is much easier for a person to understand the diagram of a decision tree than the "black box" output of a machine learning algorithm.

Machine learning encompasses both complex deep learning models and traditional statistical prediction tools like multiple regression. The statistical techniques learned in college and graduate school remain very powerful tools to analyze data. At times, a regression might be a better approach to understanding data than a deep learning algorithm. For example, identifying the risk that a patient will not effectively manage their chronic disease may be best assessed by a regression model that factors in their social determinants of health.

Win/lose outcomes. AI is best suited for win/lose situations where there is a probable right answer or outcome—for example, games such as chess or *Jeopardy!* A radiology image either does or does not show likely evidence of cancer, and the AI analysis of that image can be compared against human readings and later pathology results to determine whether the AI is correct.

AI can improve many types of win/lose situations in healthcare. As we have mentioned, AI can be applied to interpret images, or to understand speech. AI can improve the process of determining whether a prior authorization approval is needed. AI can identify inconsistencies and suggest corrections in clinical documentation.

In all these cases, there is a "true outcome" that enables us to train, test, and monitor the AI conclusions. When we don't know the truth, AI will struggle, and we will struggle to determine whether the algorithm is working well.

2.3   Categories of AI applications

The gamut of AI technologies is being applied in four major areas.

2.3.1   Extraction of data and structures

AI can be used to "understand" written and spoken language, images, video, structured and unstructured data, and combinations of these things. For example, AI can be used to extract quality measures from electronic health record data, interpret a medical image, identify faces, create a transcript from an audio file, or determine a patient's diagnosis from a collection of their health data.

AI (including "unsupervised learning" approaches, when the outcome isn't known) can identify patterns in data: the "structure" of the likely progression of an illness; access patterns to the electronic health record that indicate possible privacy violations; a series of outcomes that suggests one treatment is more effective than another; a sequence of orders that suggests a utilization management problem.

We are in the early stages of these capabilities. AI can still make significant errors when trying to distinguish signal from noise, or an organ from a tumor. But AI could potentially catch details and see patterns that elude human readers. This ability becomes particularly important as the volume and diversity of data increases.

2.3.2   Cognitive interaction

AI-enabled electronic health records (EHRs) are beginning to understand context. They can tailor the presentation of patient data and care recommendations, based on an analysis of the patient's conditions, the caregiver's preferences, the patient's preferences, the evidence, and insurance requirements. This tailoring eases the cognitive burden on the clinician. Early versions of contextual awareness are also being used to improve the systems that patients use directly, offering them the most appropriate information in an easily understandable form.

Retail applications demonstrate this interaction. They watch what you buy, identify other things you might want to buy based on the subsequent behavior of other customers who bought the things you bought, and informs you that "People like you bought these things too!"

AI-based support of cognitive interaction will be shaped by our growing understanding of how to apply behavioral economics to shape the choices that people make. The use of nudges (e.g., defaulting medication orders to the dose most likely to be correct for that patient) is an example of shaping choices.

Cognitive interaction includes conversational AI, wherein algorithms understand speech and respond with speech. To do this most effectively, the algorithms must understand not only the words spoken (in effect the transcript) but also the emotion and tone of the speech. They must recognize frustration and skepticism, for example.

2.3.3   Operational process models

AI can make processes more efficient, more tailored to a specific circumstance, more consistent and less error prone.

AI can "watch" the process of access to the narcotics cabinet in a hospital to identify possible drug diversion. AI can determine care patterns that indicate inappropriate use of clinical resources. AI can identify the correct billing codes based on the documentation of care and the tests and procedures performed (and flag when the data is incomplete), reducing claims denials.

AI-enabled systems will take population health planning to the next level of granular detail, tweaking care plans on the fly based on individual and community changes—events such as the death of a patient's spouse that might trigger depression, or a jump in pollen count that increases the risk of attacks for all the neighborhood's asthma patients. AI-enabled systems will monitor the flow of patients through the hospital and streamline activity; for example, delaying the transportation of a patient to radiology until the phlebotomist, one floor below, can complete his rounds.

In all these cases, AI is monitoring and guiding administrative and clinical processes. The AI identifies opportunities to tailor the process, intercept and correct process problems, and reduce the need for expensive labor to manage a process.

2.3.4 Clinical models

Predictive analytics will increasingly be used across a range of situations—readmissions, transitions of care, financial clearance, and medication compliance—and AI will enable analytics to learn and improve. Best practices will increasingly be defined through machine learning ("taught" by EHRs, claims, and device data) that identifies which treatments work best and flags orders for treatments that are inappropriate or ineffective. Constant monitoring of the predictions of the models, and retraining with new data when necessary, will keep the best practices current.

AI might identify potential secondary uses of medications or perform post-market surveillance and catch adverse events that didn't show up in pre-market clinical trials. It might identify which social factors—income, neighborhood, access to friends and family—have a material impact on people's health and their need for healthcare.

Healthcare AI will also show up in more mundane forms: for example, in medical equipment and devices that can monitor their own health and let technicians know when they need maintenance, are about to fail, or are improperly configured.

Across all these areas, we need to remind ourselves that an algorithm in itself is not a solution but must be integrated into other systems. A machine learning algorithm that does an exceptional job of identifying patterns of inappropriate test utilization needs to be packaged into an application that is part of clinician workflow. Incentives to use the algorithm must be in place, and clinicians must be trained on what to do with algorithm output.

2.4   Changes in AI focus

Where is your organization in its AI journey? A cross-industry survey of AI use (Deloitte Insights 2020) identified three levels of organizational AI maturity. "Starters" were just beginning to experiment; "skilled organizations" had launched multiple AI initiatives; "seasoned organizations" had become very sophisticated in their use of AI to further organizational strategies.

The report notes that the focus of AI efforts changed as organizations became more mature. Table 2.1 shows the ranking of focus areas by AI maturity. The seasoned organizations, while maintaining an overall focus on process efficiency, switched their second priority from controlling costs to creating new products and services.

Process cost reduction and efficiency may always be the foundation for AI applications in healthcare (and other industries). After all, customers judge the performance of an organization based on its core processes. Was it easy to get an appointment? Did the therapy enable me to play golf again? Do our care management processes keep people out of the hospital?

In Chapters 3 through 6, we will discuss emerging opportunities to create new products and services. For example, digital therapies can help patients manage their anxiety and depression. AI-based algorithms can provide intelligent matching of a patient's desire for a type of ambulatory care appointment with clinician availability and appointment mode (e.g., virtual vs. in-person). Chatbots can replace the need for nurses to engage in initial triage of patient complaints.

There is not always a bright line between process efficiency and new products and services. As organizations become more skilled at applying AI, they will see opportunities to expand from process efficiency to new offerings.

2.5   AI impact on healthcare business models

Digital transformation covers a very broad array of organization efforts to improve their performance and competitive position using information technology. At its core, digital transformation centers on creating new business models; organizations using digital technology to materially change what they do (e.g., evolving from a provider of healthcare to a provider of health) and how they do it (e.g., developing hospital at home programs).

As AI capabilities develop, they will become a core aspect of digital trans-formation, and AI will create new healthcare business models.

Scarcely a day goes by when we don't see an announcement of a new AI diagnostic capability in healthcare. Many involve the use of deep learning models to recognize cancers, cardiac problems, retinal diseases, bone fractures, and the like. Most of these announcements include a comparison of the AI-based diagnostic capabilities with those of human physicians. The AI usually does as well or better than the humans; in fact, in one meta-analysis (Zheng 2020), the average AI system across 69

Table 2.1   Focus of AI efforts

AI focus area	Starters	Skilled	Seasoned
Making processes more efficient	1	1 (tied)	1
Lowering costs	2	4	4
Enhancing existing products and services	3	1 (tied)	3
Creating new products and services	4	3	2

Source: Deloitte Insights 2020.

applications performed slightly better than the average human doctor in diagnostic accuracy.

But these are all research AI projects from the laboratory bench. We rarely see or hear of these AI capabilities being used at an actual patient's bedside. Why, if AI is as good as or better than human diagnosticians, do we not see it employed in actual clinical practice? Or if it is coming to that setting, why is it taking so long?

In Chapter 1 we touched on some of the systemic reasons that AI and its accompanying transformations will arrive gradually. But a major factor is the pace of maturation of the technologies themselves. The development of self-driving cars began with sensors that detect lane drift and automatically maintain a set interval from the car ahead. Today some cars can detect obstacles up ahead, sound an alarm, and slam on the brakes if the driver fails to do so. Eventually they'll learn to navigate busy city streets without hitting anything or anybody. The tipping point of transformation will arrive when they can get from point A to point B—every time—as safely as a competent human driver.

Given the relentless improvement in the technology, when might the adoption of AI segue from improving existing processes to transforming a healthcare organization's core business model? An MRI that diagnoses itself and identifies a component on the verge of failing is an operational improvement. AI-enabled analytics that can identify levers for management action to cut costs or streamline operations might be a dramatic, but still incremental, improvement.

In contrast to some other industries, healthcare organizations will come up against a distinction between using AI to improve their operations and using it to improve their core "product": patient care. The former is here now. The latter, while it may be more dramatic in the long run, is just beginning.

Several factors will shape the pace and form of AI adoption and transformation of healthcare business models. These fall into three broad categories:

IT implementation success factors. Any major IT initiative, including AI, depends on sound project management, reliable technology, and stellar user training.

Organizational competency at digital transformation factors. Some organizations have competencies that enable them to be successful across a broad portfolio of transformational digital initiatives, including AI. These competencies include change management, sound governance, good working relationships across organizational functions, a well-constructed digital architecture, and skill at managing prototypes and experiments.

Industry factors. In Chapter 1 (in the discussion of "why now"), we briefly described industry factors that have brought AI from an academic curiosity to the point of broad and deep adoption across industries. These factors will continue to evolve and shape the pace and form of AI adoption.

In addition, industry risk factors such as algorithm risk, liability, reimbursement, and regulation will have a significant impact on the degree to which AI enables new business models in healthcare. We will discuss some of these factors in Chapter 8.

In this chapter we examined AI technologies such as machine learning and robotic processing automation. We reviewed four major categories of AI applications. We discussed the potential impact of AI on healthcare business models and factors that will influence the form and adoption pace of those models.[1]

In the next four chapters, we describe a broad range of current and emerging applications of AI in healthcare.

Note

1.   An earlier version of sections 2.2.1 through 2.2.5 first appeared in T. Davenport and R. Kalakota (2019). The potential for artificial intelligence in healthcare. *Future Healthcare Journal*, 6(2): 94–8. The version is reused with permission.

References

Bush, J. (2018). How AI is taking the scut work out of health care. *Harvard Business Review*, March 5. https://hbr.org/2018/03/how-ai-is-taking-the-scut-work-out-of-health-care.

Davenport, T., Hongsermeier, T. and Alba, K. (2018). Using AI to improve electronic health records. *Harvard Business Review*, December 13. https://hbr.org/2018/12/using-ai-to-improve-electronic-health-records.

Davenport, T. and Kalakota, R. (2019). The potential for artificial intelligence in healthcare. *Future Healthcare Journal*, 6(2): 94–8. http://doi.org/10.7861/futurehosp.6-2-94.

Deloitte Insights (2018). State of AI in the enterprise. *Deloitte*. https://www2.deloitte.com/content/dam/insights/us/articles/4780_Stateof-AI-in-the-enterprise/AICognitiveSurvey2018_Infographic.pdf.

Deloitte Insights (2020). State of AI in the enterprise, 3rd edition. *Deloitte*. https://www2.deloitte.com/content/dam/insights/us/articles/6462_state-of-ai-in-the-enterprise/DI_State-of-AI.pdf.

Fakoor, R., Ladhak, F., Nazi, A. and Huber, M. (2013). Using deep learning to enhance cancer diagnosis and classification. The 30th International Conference on Machine Learning. https://www.researchgate.net/publication/281857285_Using_deep_learning_to_enhance_cancer_diagnosis_and_classification.

Hussain, A., Malik, A., Halim, M.U. and Ali, A.M. (2014). The use of robotics in surgery: a review. *International Journal of Clinical Practice*, 68(11): 1376–82. http://doi.org/10.1111/ijcp.12492.

Lee, S.I., Celik, S., Logsdon, B.A., et al. (2018). A machine learning approach to integrate big data for precision medicine in acute myeloid leukemia. *Nature Communications*, 9(1): 42. https://doi.org/10.1038/s41467-017-02465-5.

Metz, C. (2021). The robot surgeon will see you now. *New York Times*, April 30. https://www.nytimes.com/2021/04/30/technology/robot-surgery-surgeon.html.

Morse, S. (2021). Microsoft doubles healthcare market with acquisition of Nuance. *Healthcare Finance News*, April 13. https://www.healthcarefinancenews.com/news/microsoft-doubles-healthcare-market-acquisition-nuance.

Sordo, M. (2002). Introduction to neural networks in healthcare. *OpenClinical*. http://www.openclinical.org/docs/int/neuralnetworks011.pdf.

Vial, A., Stirling, D., Field, M., et al. (2018). The role of deep learning and radiomic feature extraction in cancer-specific predictive modelling: a review. *Translational Cancer Research*, 7: 803–16.

Zheng, Q., Yang, L., Zeng, B., et al. (2020). Artificial intelligence performance in detecting tumor metastasis from medical radiology imaging: a systematic review and meta-analysis. *EClinicalMedicine*, December 25. http://doi.org/10.1016/j.eclinm.2020.100669.

3 AI for diagnosis and treatment

3.1   Introduction

Ways to apply artificial intelligence to the diagnosis and treatment of disease are proliferating so quickly that between the time we're writing this chapter and the time you are reading it, thousands—or perhaps tens of thousands—of new papers will have been published. In September 2021 alone, more than 1,800 new journal citations including the term "artificial intelligence" appeared on PubMed, the U.S. National Library of Medicine's central publication database. They span a stunning variety of applications. Just a small sample:

- In a study of upper GI endoscopy, AI reduced the "miss rate" for finding gastric neoplasms from 27% to 6% compared with routine review by radiologists. (Wu 2021)
- An AI-based screening tool was about 90% accurate in distinguishing Covid-19 patients from healthy controls by measuring tiny variations in the sound of their voices as they sustained a single vowel sound. (Vahedian-Azimi 2021)
- A machine learning algorithm detected Parkinson's disease with 95% accuracy by analyzing "micro-expressions"—extremely subtle movements of facial muscles—in videos of people with and without Parkinson's. (Ali 2021)

Clearly, attempting to keep up with these developments in their entirety would be futile. Fortunately, it's not necessary. As we discuss elsewhere, healthcare organizations will rarely adopt individual applications of AI, but will instead encounter them as a feature of a product or system— either as an upgrade to what they already have or as a new capability. Most of these research discoveries will never even find their way into commercial products, though every success (and every published or unpublished failure) contributes in some way to the eventual AI infrastructure that will transform how we approach the practice of medicine.

However, we think it's important for healthcare leaders to understand the potential scope of AI involvement in diagnosis and treatment so they can begin to grasp the magnitude of the changes that are headed our way. It may be useful to classify these applications into several broad categories.

3.2   Interpreting image data

Radiology has been the first medical specialty to benefit significantly from AI, which can analyze images pixel by pixel and sometimes detect potential problems unseeable by the trained human eye. Almost all the healthcare applications in this category make use of the relatively new AI technology called deep learning. It often works extremely well at prediction or classification tasks. As of early 2021, the U.S. Food and Drug Administration (FDA) had cleared more than 100 AI algorithms for radiology (Allen 2021).

Modern imaging modalities produce too much information for a human to process efficiently: hundreds or even thousands of images for each scan. Because the images are digital, a properly trained algorithm can scan them quickly and find anomalies for a radiologist to look at more closely. An application to detect lung cancer on CT scans—a joint venture between Northwestern University in Chicago, Google, and several other institutions—discovered a patient's disease a year or more before it would have been discovered by human readers (Ardila 2019).

Even for routine imaging like chest x-rays, AI can help flag suspicious areas and may be especially helpful to primary care physicians who don't get as much practice looking at images (Ueda 2021).

In the U.S.A., almost a third of radiology practices were using some form of AI by 2020, according to a survey by the American College of Radiologists (Allen 2021). Of those who weren't yet using AI-based tools, 20 percent were planning to invest soon. Experts say fears of AI taking over for radiologists are overblown. Instead, AI is more likely to remove tedium, increase accuracy, and allow radiologists to apply their skills, experience, and judgment where they are most needed (Siwicki 2021).

One issue that must be addressed in radiology AI is the narrow scope of applications. A radiologist, for example, could use an algorithm called OsteoDetect to help diagnose a wrist fracture in an image, but what about the many other types of fractures that so far have no algorithm? Or the other types of imaging done every day that have nothing to do with bones? It would be difficult to build a complete clinical practice or an efficient clinical workflow around the single-purpose AI-assisted options available today.

Radiology associations around the world are beginning to address the issue of creating more and broader use cases and clinician workflows. The American College of Radiology, for example, has created a Data Science Institute (DSI) to encourage, validate, and integrate AI use cases. The DSI works with individual radiologists who develop algorithms as well as vendors of devices and software. The goal is to integrate the use cases into a broader platform for clinician workflow and decision-making called CAR/DS (Computer-Assisted Reporting/Decision Support).

In the U.K., the Royal College of Radiologists has issued guidance on how to interface AI applications into radiology data standards and clinical workflows. The healthcare industry will need other efforts like this to deal with the integration of dozens of narrow AI algorithms into broader processes and workflows.

3.3   Analyzing sound

AI algorithms can learn to analyze audio data as well as images and video, and can detect patterns and variations that humans can't hear.

One potential predictor of dementia, whether from Alzheimer's disease (AD) or other causes, is subtle changes in vocal quality and speech, according to a deep learning analysis of data from the famous Framingham Heart Study, which lasted for decades. The researchers used voice recordings of more than 1,200 study participants who also had neuropsychological evaluations. After training two algorithms to hear the vocal patterns of patients known to have normal brain function and patients with confirmed Alzheimer's, the researchers tested how easily they classified patients who weren't part of the training set. While performance wasn't perfect, the algorithms were able to distinguish between the two groups well enough to warrant further research. Early screening for dementia through voice analysis would be inexpensive and easy on patients, and accuracy might improve with better recording technology (Xue 2021).

3.4   Mining the genome

Finding patterns in mountains of data is one of AI's strong suits. Genomic data represents an entire Himalaya-sized mountain range. AI can show us clues to our medical future hidden in the complex relationships among our genes. With warning, we may be able to prevent disastrous outcomes from certain diseases and better prepare ourselves for others. For example:

Who will develop severe Covid-19? One of the biggest mysteries of the pandemic is why some people have no symptoms at all and others end up in an ICU on a ventilator. A paper published in *Nature* describes a deep learning algorithm that discovered a specific genetic variation in patients' T-cell receptors—an element of their immune systems—that put them more at risk of severe Covid. If this type of analysis moved out of the lab to be applied to patients' genetic information, they would be warned about their heightened risk and take extra care to avoid becoming infected (Sidhom 2021).

Who will develop Alzheimer's disease? No one has discovered "the gene for Alzheimer's," though several gene variations have been associated with an elevated risk of developing the disease, the world's sixth leading cause of death. An AI framework analyzed several existing databases of genetic information on patients with confirmed AD and identified a complex of several genes associated with inflammation that correlate with the development of the disease (Beebe-Wang 2021).

Discovering new uses for old drugs. Every aspect of AD involves heartbreak, and that includes the many failed efforts to find drugs to treat it. Researchers at Harvard have devised a machine learning application they call DRIAD—Drug Repurposing in Alzheimer's Disease—that does analysis at the level of individual genes to identify existing drugs that might have some effect on the brains of patients with Alzheimer's. The algorithm uses mRNA information from human brains at various stages of AD—derived from several large research databases—and compares it against lists of genes whose expression is known to be affected by certain drugs. Their initial use of the application turned up 80 existing drugs, many now used to fight cancer, that act on the genes under investigation (Rodriguez 2021).

3.5   Sifting through EHR and monitor data

A hospital stay generates enormous amounts of data, especially when patients undergo procedures or are hooked up to monitoring equipment. Clinicians usually use only a small amount of it during the stay, but AI could significantly expand its usefulness. These types of applications typically use more conventional types of machine learning models, which can either predict outcomes (supervised learning) or find hidden patterns in data (unsupervised learning).

Bates et al. (2021) examined a wide range of promising initiatives that apply AI to EHR data to improve the safety of healthcare. They include:

- Detection and prediction of hospital acquired infections
- Identification of potential adverse drug reactions and prediction of the risk of an adverse reaction
- Identification of patients at high risk of venous thromboembolisms
- Prediction of the potential surgical complications
- Early detection of pressure ulcers
- Determination of the risk of a patient fall
- Prediction of decompensation due following complications of trauma surgery
- Reduction in diagnostic errors through suggestions of potential diagnoses.

Following are some examples:

Predicting and averting crises. During hospital stays, subtle cues to impending disaster may exist in patients' vital signs and other routinely collected information. Applying AI may reveal these cues that busy humans miss, allowing clinicians to adjust medications or otherwise take steps to prevent the crisis entirely. It's relatively common, for example, to use machine learning models to predict the onset of sepsis. In addition, a multinational team of researchers used machine learning to develop an early-warning system that uses measurements from multiple organ systems to predict 90 percent of circulatory-failure events, with 82 percent identified more than two hours in advance (Hyland 2020).

At the University of Michigan, researchers have created machine learning algorithms that predict the likelihood of ICU transfer or death for patients in surgical rehab units and Covid-19 units, using lab and vital sign data from the electronic health record, heart rate variability data from monitors, and image data (Cummings 2021).

Predicting post-operative complications. What if we could predict with great precision which patients are at risk of complications after surgery, and take steps beforehand to prevent those complications? A recent study took data from more than five million post-operative patients over six years—with up to 76 data points per patient—and used it to train three deep neural network models, using different levels of detail for each. Researchers held out data from patients at a single medical center to test the models after training. All three models outperformed existing surgical risk prediction methods, and more details increase accuracy (Bonde 2021). These types of tools could also help surgeons make highly individualized risk assessments for each patient, and help patients better understand the risks for their particular case.

Identifying optimal treatment approaches. Healthcare providers and purchasers place a premium on ensuring that care delivery is "evidence based." In other words, the results of clinical trials and rigorous reviewed and published studies of best care practices are reflected in the day-to-day delivery of care. Leveraging AI to analyze very large datasets will dramatically expand the evidence base beyond the traditional approaches of clinical trials, and review committees of respected specialists (Cleary 2019).

The use of "real world evidence" to guide patient care is still very much in its early stages. However, several categories of initiatives can leverage AI to analyze the evidence:

- Comparative effectiveness: comparing the outcomes of patients who received one approach to treatment with patients who received a different approach
- Post-market surveillance: monitoring the data, in real time, to determine if there is evidence that a medication or device is causing harm
- New uses of existing medications: assessing whether a medication used for one purpose may be leading to improved health in other, unanticipated clinical situations.

In addition to diagnosis and treatment, AI-based analyses of very large sets of clinical data have potential applications in identifying candidates for clinical trials and detecting disease outbreaks at their earliest stages.

3.6   Helping clinicians deal with EHRs

Most clinicians would agree that electronic health records are more useful than paper ones, but they can still point to a long list of ways that EHRs thwart their ability to care for patients. It's too hard to find the most important information for a given encounter and too easy to enter information in the wrong place or select the wrong choice on a pull-down menu. AI can help in a multitude of ways.

Smart scribes. Human scribes—trained to take clinicians' dictation as they work and then transfer the information to the EHR—have been a common workaround for getting information into EHRs. Speech recognition and natural language processing can streamline that process even more by channeling clinician utterances directly into the appropriate place in the record. This capability is in development or on offer in several widely used EHR systems.

Deciphering acronyms. "RA" in a medical note could be "rheumatoid arthritis" or "right atrium." "CC" could be "critical care" or "cubic centimeter" or even "chief complaint." Human readers usually have little trouble decoding such ambiguities depending on context, but computers have struggled. However, deep learning algorithms can grasp the needed context to translate abbreviations correctly, which makes the EHR easier to search and helps make clinicians' notes intelligible to lay readers (Skreta 2021).

Simplifying search and data entry. EHRs must serve many masters, of which the top two are usually the billing department (to get paid for services provided) and the legal department (to document those services in the event of a lawsuit). Clinicians often feel like (and are) an afterthought, but AI can potentially recast EHR information to be useful to them by arranging it to reflect the way clinicians think. For example, a research team at the Massachusetts Institute of Technology and Beth Israel Deaconess Hospital in Boston created "MedKnowts," an AI application that sorts through EHRs and finds data relevant to the problem at hand. If the application sees "diabetes" as the clinician types, it displays a "diabetes card" showing medications, lab values, and notes from past visits or other records that are relevant to the patient's diabetes treatment (Zewe 2021).

Keeping care plans on track. Similarly, AI could be employed to customize care plans to the specific needs of a particular patient—not just a standardized sheet of aftercare instructions but one that recognizes that the patient has both diabetes and mild cognitive impairment and may need routine reminders to take his medication, or that he lives alone without a car and may need help arranging transportation to the next appointment.

3.7   The path to market

AI for diagnosis and treatment is eventually going to impact every healthcare organization in one or more of these categories as vendors incorporate these capabilities into existing products or develop new ones. As noted elsewhere, some applications will need regulatory approval depending on the extent to which they are directly involved in determining the details of patient care. The U.S. FDA classifies certain applications of AI as "medical devices" and has regulated them accordingly. Europe does the same through its CE Mark. The FDA maintains a database of approved devices, called "Artificial Intelligence and Machine Learning (AI/ML)-Enabled Medical Devices," which lists both the products and their manufacturers (FDA Digital Health Center of Excellence 2021).

A few applications that the FDA has approved include:

GI Genius (April 2021). A device that helps gastroenterologists detect suspicious lesions in real time during a colonoscopy. Designed to be compatible with many FDA-approved video endoscopy systems, it draws a green box around areas that it thinks need closer inspection. In a randomized controlled trial of 700 patients, colonoscopy enhanced with GI Genius identified lab-confirmed adenomas or carcinomas in 55 percent of patients, compared with 42 percent using standard colonoscopy: an observed difference of 13 percent.

Caption Guidance (February 2020). An AI-enabled interface that guides users through cardiac ultrasound image acquisition to ensure that the images and video clips are of diagnostic quality. The interface provides real-time feedback on potential image quality, can auto-capture video clips, and automatically saves the best video clip acquired from a particular view. The algorithm stops far short of offering clinical opinions: a cardiologist uses the images to evaluate the patient (FDA Press Office 2020).

IDx-DR (April 2018). A software program that uses an AI algorithm to analyze images of the retina to detect signs of diabetic retinopathy and refer patients for further evaluation.

Regulatory clearance alone can't guarantee that an AI-based application will always work as billed in clinical use. A 2021 commentary in the *Journal of the American College of Radiology* recommended that clinicians be able to answer these questions when considering adopting AI. They apply equally to all specialties, not just radiology (Allen 2021):

1. What is the scope of products that are available for my intended use?
2. How were the models trained and how were they validated?
3. Once purchased, will an AI application perform as expected in my practice? How can I monitor the performance of the model after deployment?

3.8   Focusing clinical AI adoption initiatives: centers of excellence

Clinical innovations often find their way into a healthcare institution from the bottom up, and AI is likely to follow that pattern. A clinician will read a paper or see a meeting presentation or talk to a colleague, and the next thing you know (or perhaps don't know), they are exploring ways to develop or adopt an AI-based application in their department. While such initiative is to be applauded in some ways, a piecemeal approach to AI is at best not an efficient way to reap the full benefits of such a potentially revolutionary development. At worst, it can create problems with data governance or even open the institution to malpractice risk that it may not be aware of until it's too late.

How should healthcare organizations begin to make sense of AI developments, and to strategize for their eventual adoption? One approach is to establish an AI Center of Excellence (CoE). These are increasingly common in business organizations, but only now emerging in healthcare providers (Davenport 2019). While this catchphrase can encompass a variety of functions, we define it as a method of establishing a focal point for AI interest, so that bottom-up initiatives will have a home and leaders will be able to monitor and manage them to the extent needed. The establishment of such a center may prompt other AI champions to emerge and allow them to coordinate their efforts.

Such a CoE can evaluate specific applications (and even create them, if the organization has the necessary expertise), begin to compile an institutional AI wish list to direct further investigation, and develop and execute an overall AI strategy.

We discuss AI CoEs in more detail in Chapter 9. Most of these centers will be focused on ensuring sound management of internal AI initiatives. Some centers will have an expanded goal of bringing AI solutions to the healthcare industry, especially if their health system has:

- An established, excellent national and global brand
- Partnerships with technology companies interested in developing AI products and services
- An innovation funding program that invests in digital health startups

- An effective technology transfer function to move intellectual property from "the lab" to industry.

The Cleveland Clinic, for example, established its Center for Clinical Artificial Intelligence in 2019, after AI initiatives began "popping up all over the place," according to Chris Donovan, Executive Director of Enterprise Information Management and Analytics. His group is trying to facilitate the bottom-up efforts to develop and deploy AI, while also providing governance approaches.

The clinic has multiple AI projects in progress at any given time, ranging from algorithms to predict outcomes and readmission risk (Hilton 2020) to assessing mortality risk in the pediatric ICU (Baloglu 2021) to identifying the make and model of implanted artificial joints using simple x-ray images (Karnuta 2021).

Having the center facilitates functions that are useful across all AI initiatives, such as standardizing preparation of data. Donovan's group provides useful datasets to all AI projects. For example, a simple measurement like blood pressure can vary depending on whether the patient is standing, sitting, or lying down. Effective data collection requires that detail to be captured at the time of the measurement.

The Mayo Clinic has established an AI Factory, in partnership with Google, to accelerate the development of AI software. The Factory has 60 projects underway, some of which have sparked the creation of new companies (McCormick 2021).

Example projects include:

- Using de-identified data and images to develop an algorithm that can help clinicians create radiation therapy plans for cancer patients more quickly and efficiently
- Analyzing radiology images for body composition markers that can indicate underlying chronic conditions.

The startup companies formed through the AI Factory include:

Anumana, which will focus on developing and commercializing AI-enabled algorithms for early detection of "silent" cardiovascular conditions like a weak heart pump, silent arrhythmias, or a thickened heart pump, before they pose a risk of stroke or heart failure.

Lucem Health, which will focus on ingesting and connecting remote patient telemetry devices with the algorithms developed by Mayo Clinic and partners. The company also will help Mayo integrate diagnostic insights generated by these algorithms into clinical workflows.

Increasing numbers of eminent medical institutions have established AI CoEs or are wrapping AI into existing digital health centers. They typically primarily address diagnosis and treatment issues, though some may also deal with administrative AI applications. Some focus on specific disease areas, such as cancer. Others look at broader health issues. Intermountain Healthcare, a not-for-profit system of 24 hospitals based in Utah, formed its Data Science and Artificial Intelligence Center of Excellence in 2021 with a focus on ethical standards—fighting bias, ensuring transparency, and protecting privacy—as AI and machine learning algorithms proliferate across healthcare (Miliard 2021).

Such CoEs may persist over the long run, or may be merged into other groups as AI becomes more commonplace in healthcare organizations. It seems likely, however, that a coherent and coordinated organizational approach to AI during this era of rapid change will make its deployment both more successful and more efficient.

We've looked at several ways that AI is likely to change the way we diagnose and treat some diseases. In the next chapter, we'll take a closer look at how AI is being used in the development of drugs, medical devices, and entire "smart" facilities.

References

Ali, M.R., Myers, T., Wagner, E., Ratnu, H., Dorsey, E.R. and Hoque, E. (2021). Facial expressions can detect Parkinson's disease: preliminary evidence from videos collected online. *NPJ Digital Medicine*, 4(1): 129. http://doi.org/10.1038/s41746-021-00502-8.

Allen, B., Dreyer, K., Stibolt, R. Jr., et al. (2021). Evaluation and real-world performance monitoring of artificial intelligence models in clinical practice purchase: try it, buy it, check it [published online ahead of print, September 29]. *Journal of the American College of Radiology*, 18(11): 1489–96. http://doi.org/10.1016/j.jacr.2021.08.022.

Ardila, D., Kiraly, A.P., Bharadwaj, S., et al. (2019). End-to-end lung cancer screening with three-dimensional deep learning on low-dose chest computed tomography. *Nature Medicine*, 25(6): 954–61. http://doi.org/10.1038/s41591-019-0447-x [published correction appears in *Nature Medicine* (2019), 25(8): 1319].

Baloglu, O., Nagy, M., Ezetendu, C., Latifi, S.Q. and Nazha, A. (2021). Simplified pediatric index of mortality 3 score by explainable machine learning algorithm. *Critical Care Explanations*, 3(10): e0561. http://doi.org/10.1097/CCE.0000000000000561.

Bates, D.W., Levine, D., Syrowatka, A., et al. (2021). The potential of artificial intelligence to improve patient safety: a scoping review. *NPJ Digital Medicine*, 4(1): 54. http://doi.org/10.1038/s41746-021-00423-6.

Beebe-Wang, N., Celik, S., Weinberger, E., et al. (2021). Unified AI framework to uncover deep interrelationships between gene expression and Alzheimer's disease neuropathologies. *Nature Communications*, 12(1): 5369. http://doi.org/10.1038/s41467-021-25680-7.

Bonde, A., Varadarajan, K.M., Bonde, N., et al. (2021). Assessing the utility of deep neural networks in predicting postoperative surgical complications: a retrospective study. *Lancet Digital Health*, 3(8): e471–e485. http://doi.org/10.1016/S2589-7500(21)00084-4.

Cleary, M. (2019). Artificial intelligence: the key to unlocking novel real-world data? ISPOR, *Value & Outcomes Spotlight*, March/April. https://www.ispor.org/publications/journals/value-outcomes-spotlight/abstract/march-april-2019/artificial-intelligence-the-key-to-unlocking-novel-real-world-data.

Cummings, B.C., Ansari, S., Motyka, J.R., et al. (2021). Predicting intensive care transfers and other unforeseen events: analytic model validation study and comparison to existing methods. *JMIR Medical Informatics*, 9(4): e25066. http://doi.org/10.2196/25066.

Davenport, T.H. and Dasgupta, S. (2019). How to set up an AI center of excellence. *Harvard Business Review*, January 16. https://hbr.org/2019/01/how-to-set-up-an-ai-center-of-excellence.

FDA Digital Health Center of Excellence (2021). Artificial intelligence and machine learning (AI/ML)-enabled medical devices. Updated September 22, 2021. https://www.fda.gov/medical-devices/software-medical-device-samd/artificial-intelligence-and-machine-learning-aiml-enabled-medical-devices.

FDA Press Office (2020). FDA authorizes marketing of first cardiac ultrasound software that uses artificial intelligence to guide user. Press release, February 7.

Hilton, C.B., Milinovich, A., Felix, C., et al. (2020). Personalized predictions of patient outcomes during and after hospitalization using artificial intelligence. *NPJ Digital Medicine*, 3: 51. http://doi.org/10.1038/s41746-020-0249-z.

Hyland, S.L., Faltys, M., Hüser, M., et al. (2020). Early prediction of circulatory failure in the intensive care unit using machine learning. *Nature Medicine*, 26(3): 364–73. http://doi.org/10.1038/s41591-020-0789-4.

Karnuta, J.M., Haeberle, H.S., Luu, B.C., et al. (2021). Artificial Intelligence to identify arthroplasty implants from radiographs of the hip. *Journal of Arthroplasty*, 36(7S): S290–S294. http://doi.org/10.1016/j.arth.2020.11.015.

McCormick, J. (2021). Mayo Clinic, others use 'AI Factories' to speed AI development. *Wall Street Journal*, May 18. https://www.wsj.com/articles/mayo-clinic
-others-use-ai-factories-to-speed-ai-development-11621330202.

Miliard, M. (2021). Intermountain launches new AI center to guide ethical
deployments and prevent care disparities. *Healthcare IT News*, November 18.

Rodriguez, S., Hug, C., Todorov, P., et al. (2021). Machine learning identifies candidates for drug repurposing in Alzheimer's disease. *Nature Communications*,
12(1): 1033. http://doi.org/10.1038/s41467-021-21330-0.

Sidhom, J.W. and Baras, A.S. (2021). Deep learning identifies antigenic determinants of severe SARS-CoV-2 infection within T-cell repertoires. *Scientific
Reports*, 11(1): 14275. https://doi.org/10.1038/s41598-021-93608-8.

Siwicki, B. (2021). Mass General Brigham and the future of AI in radiology.
Healthcare IT News, May 10.

Skreta, M., Arbabi, A., Wang, J., et al. (2021). Automatically disambiguating
medical acronyms with ontology-aware deep learning. *Nature Communications*,
12(1): 5319. http://doi.org/10.1038/s41467-021-25578-4.

Ueda, D., Yamamoto, A., Shimazaki, A., et al. (2021). Artificial
intelligence-supported lung cancer detection by multi-institutional readers
with multi-vendor chest radiographs: a retrospective clinical validation study.
BMC Cancer, 21(1): 1120. http://doi.org/10.1186/s12885-021-08847-9.

Vahedian-Azimi, A., Keramatfar, A., Asiaee, M., Atashi, S.S. and Nourbakhsh, M.
(2021). Do you have COVID-19? An artificial intelligence-based screening tool
for COVID-19 using acoustic parameters. *Journal of the Acoustical Society of
America*, 150(3): 1945. http://doi.org/10.1121/10.0006104.

Wu, L., Shang, R., Sharma, P., et al. (2021). Effect of a deep learning-based system
on the miss rate of gastric neoplasms during upper gastrointestinal endoscopy:
a single-centre, tandem, randomised controlled trial. *Lancet Gastroenterology
& Hepatology*, 6(9): 700–708. http://doi.org/10.1016/S2468-1253(21)00216-8.

Xue, C., Karjadi, C., Paschalidis, I.C., Au, R. and Kolachalama, V.B. (2021).
Detection of dementia on voice recordings using deep learning: a Framingham
Heart Study. *Alzheimer's Research & Therapy*, 13(1): 146. http://doi.org/10
.1186/s13195-021-00888-3.

Zewe, A. (2021). Toward a smarter electronic health record. *MIT News Office*,
September 23. https://news.mit.edu/2021/medknowts-electronic-health
-record-0923.

4   AI-based drugs, devices, facilities, and the like

4.1   Introduction

The future will feature drugs designed by AI, medical devices that enable AI to interpret sensor data, smart exam and hospital rooms, smart ambulances, smart wearables, smart pills, and multiple other smart healthcare tools. The present ... not so much. There are a few somewhat smart devices on the market, and AI has played a part in the development of some drugs and vaccines.

Nonetheless, it's useful for healthcare executives to think now about how AI will affect drugs and devices and thus the care that their organizations will be able and expected to provide. While it may be too early to offer most of these innovations now, your ability to offer them in the future may depend on the investments and agreements you make today: in facilities, in software and communications networks, and in partnerships (with payers, other providers, and technology developers) that are designed to take full advantage of these new capabilities.

4.2   Current and future AI-enabled drug discovery and development

Although AI hasn't had much of an influence yet on drug development, the technology could dramatically reshape healthcare by cutting the cost for developing highly effective treatments for important diseases, and drastically reducing the development time and cost. The Tufts Center for

Drug Development estimates that the average drug approved by the U.S. Food and Drug Administration (FDA) requires over ten years and over $2 billion in costs, so there is a major need for improvement.

Pharma firms are beginning to use AI, at least on the margins, to develop and test new drugs (Freedman 2019). Some had partnerships with the much-touted IBM Watson AI project, but those have all been discontinued. Big Pharma firms like Pfizer are using AI for marketing, sales, pharmacovigilance, and some clinical trial developments. Novartis, AstraZeneca, and a few other large companies have ambitious development programs using AI as a central tool. Some midsize firms, including Regeneron Pharmaceuticals, are using AI more aggressively to explore the role of genetics in identifying drug targets.

AstraZeneca (AZ) is using large datasets and machine learning to predict and rank which molecules might have an impact on disease targets. They're in the process of dramatically speeding up the drug development process with this approach. The next step in the process is to synthesize the molecules in the lab, and tools like protein folding prediction are making it possible to also speed molecule synthesis. Pathologists are using AI to accelerate the process of tissue and cell analysis by up to 30 percent. Automation technologies, both physical robots and process automation, help to accelerate the repeated cycles of generating, analyzing, and testing new compounds. And AZ is using federated electronic health record data to speed up clinical trials.

Researchers have used machine learning to discover whether existing drugs can be repurposed for applications other than those originally intended and approved. AI can also be used for post-market surveillance of side effects or unanticipated problems, typically through automated reviews of the medical literature and by analyzing electronic health record and other "real world" data. Vendors such as Iris and Aidence offer software to aid in that process.

Some smaller and startup pharma firms are using AI to redesign core drug development processes. Some are partnering with established pharma firms. They use AI to simulate the interaction of molecules *in silico* (i.e., on a computer) and to assess the potential of different molecules for their impact on a target. A molecule that has no impact on the target in these simulations can be quickly ruled out as a candidate for a new drug, shrinking the portfolio of possibilities to those that are most likely to be effective.

Exscientia, a U.K.-based startup, announced in 2021 that it had developed a cancer immunotherapy treatment using AI-based design. It had previously announced an AI-designed drug for treating obsessive/compulsive disorder, in partnership with Sumitomo Dainippon Pharma in Japan. The company has several drugs in clinical trials, putting it ahead of many other AI-fueled startups.

Insilico Medicine, based in Hong Kong, announced in 2021 that it had identified a new target in cells that is linked to pulmonary fibrosis, and designed a new molecule to address the target and treat the disease. The design phase took 18 months and cost about $2 million—far faster and cheaper than traditional methods.

In the U.S.A., Berg Health, a Boston-based startup, has partnered with AZ and other firms to use AI to design new drugs based on analysis of biomarker data. The company has a drug to treat glioblastoma, a form of brain cancer, in clinical trials.

It's too early to state with confidence that AI-based drug development can bring new drugs to market faster and with less expense. But the AI-driven approaches used by these startups appear to be an effective way to go about the process. If the startups succeed, they are likely to be acquired by Big Pharma firms.

Other new developments in AI and biology could have a major effect on drug development. For example, in 2020, Alphabet's DeepMind AI R&D unit claimed it had developed an algorithm to accomplish one of the most complex feats in biology: accurately predicting the shape of protein folding from the genetic sequences that encode the proteins. While it's still too early to know the exact influence of this development on understanding disease and developing treatments, it could be dramatic. As a *Fortune* magazine article put it, the discovery

> … could prove transformative for much of humanity. Proteins are the basic building blocks of life and the mechanism behind most biological processes. Being able to predict their structure could revolutionize our understanding of disease and lead to new, more targeted pharmaceuticals for disorders

from cancer to Alzheimer's disease. It will likely accelerate the time it takes to bring new medicines to market, potentially shaving years and hundreds of millions of dollars in costs from drug development, and potentially saving lives as a result. (Kahn 2020)

At least one vaccine development firm, Moderna Therapeutics, is making extensive use of AI (MIT Sloan Management Review 2021). While it did not use AI for core development of its mRNA-based Covid-19 vaccine, the company employed AI in a variety of tasks associated with preclinical development and clinical trials. Robotic process automation and machine learning models helped produce enough small-scale mRNA to support the research, confirmed that DNA sequences were correct, optimized DNA sequences for production, and optimized clinical trial planning. AI accelerated the production of the vaccine, no doubt saving thousands of lives, if not millions. Pfizer, which collaborated with the German firm BioNTech on clinical trials for its mRNA vaccine, also used AI in some aspects of the trials, such as integrating and testing data. BioNTech announced in late 2020 that it would collaborate with British firm InstaDeep on an AI innovation lab (BioNTech 2020).

4.3   AI-enabled precision medical treatments

Precision medicine—treatments based on a patient's genetic makeup—is emerging slowly and offers several opportunities for AI to assist. Precision medicine is particularly relevant to cancer treatment, where certain drugs are effective (or not) depending on the genetic makeup of the patient's tumor cells. Given the complexity of the human genome and the multiplicity of cancer drugs and clinical trials, oncologists and their patients need help from AI to determine which diagnostic test and which treatments are appropriate for a patient.

Imagine, for example, that you're a patient being treated for prostate cancer and the treatment is not going well. Desperate, you've signed up for alerts on new treatments. You receive this perplexing press release, which says, in part:

> Foundation Medicine, Inc. [FMI] today announced that it has received approval from the U.S. Food and Drug Administration (FDA) for FoundationOne˚CDx to be used as a companion diagnostic for LYNPARZA˚ (olaparib), which was

also approved today in the U.S. for adult patients with deleterious or suspected deleterious germline or somatic homologous recombination repair (HRR) gene-mutated metastatic castration-resistant prostate cancer (mCRPC) who have progressed following prior treatment with enzalutamide or abiraterone … . "This therapy and companion diagnostic approval underscores the value of comprehensive genomic profiling in advanced cancer patients as it validates our ability to identify alterations in the 14 HRR pathway genes within FoundationOne CDx's 324 gene panel that indicate a patient may be eligible for treatment with Lynparza, a process not possible through single gene or hot spot testing," said Brian Alexander, M.D., M.P.H., chief medical officer at Foundation Medicine. (Foundation Medicine 2020)

Imagine that you had to decide—even with the help of a knowledgeable physician—whether to take the recommended diagnostic test, let alone the related drug.

Dr. Rana McKay, an oncologist at the University of California San Diego Medical Center (UCSD), told us that the amount of information can be overwhelming not only for the patient, but also for the general practitioner or the average oncologist:

Advances in technology have led to overwhelming amount of data on tumor biology, patterns of disease, and outcomes for patients. How do you take all that information and distill it down into a therapy choice for each patient? At an academic cancer center like UCSD with robust precision medicine program and institutional Molecular Tumor Board there are tremendous resources available in helping better interpret clinical-grade sequencing data, but such resources may not be readily available across all oncology practices.

Companies like Foundation Medicine provide genomic sequencing of cancer tissue samples for biomarkers that may aid treatment. Foundation Medicine is using its vast genomic database and partnering with biopharma organizations to try to translate findings about genes and mutations into treatment options and clinical trial possibilities for cancer patients.

Foundation Medicine tries to match patients with treatment options and trials. As described in the press release above, it partners with pharma firms that have developed cancer treatment drugs to validate the tests' ability to detect specific mutations and match appropriate patients to approved and targeted therapies. It generates an AI-enabled report for a patient's oncologist about the genomic mutations present in the patient's tumor or blood (for example, BRCA2, commonly found in breast cancer, but also sometimes present in prostate cancer), the FDA-approved therapeutic options (for example, olaparib and rucaparib, both recommended for treatment of cancers with BRCA2 mutations), and other genomic biomarker findings of possible clinical relevance. The report also lists clinical trials a patient may be eligible for in which the treatment options are being tested. (AI is not the only source of expertise, however: the report is curated by genomics experts and pathologists.)

FMI is aggregating de-identified patient genomic data from its own tests, and it plans to use that data at some point to train machine learning models to recommend treatments and trials. But Priti Hegde, FMI's Chief Scientific Officer, said in an interview that there is more human learning than machine learning at work today:

> We are gathering data on the response of patients to particular cancer treatments. But that takes years to play out. Typically, one needs millions of cases to train machine learning models, but so far, we have only thousands or in some cases hundreds of thousands. We do use systems to recommend treatments and trials, but they are a rules-based approach that represents the knowledge generated from our large database and from the scientists at FMI.

Dr. Hegde, in our view, is establishing a high standard for the amount of required data for machine learning. It may be possible to develop effective machine learning models with fewer cases. It may also be that new AI methods will enable training on smaller amounts of data or even synthetic data.

Dr. McKay of UCSD said that the companies try to make their reports provider-friendly, but they are not specific to particular types of cancer, and they do not account for the patient's personal cancer history, including prior treatments. She notes that though genetic screening companies are making progress at explaining treatment options, oncologists still need to know a good deal about the genomics of cancer to use the information effectively in patient care. As AI applications become more sophisticated, they may improve both the effectiveness of their recommendations and their ability to explain those recommendations to primary care physicians and patients.

4.4   Current and future AI-enabled medical devices

AI will eventually enable smart devices for many healthcare applications: longer-term and everyday health monitoring, diagnosis, and support. "Medical device" is a confusing term when it comes to AI, because it can mean either a physical device, controlled by software, or simply a software application. The U.S. FDA regulates both categories under the blanket term "Artificial Intelligence/Machine Learning-Based Software as a Medical Device." In that broad sense there are many AI-enabled devices intended to support diagnosis (medical image recognition is an example), some of which we discuss in Chapter 3. Some AI-enabled devices support health maintenance or the management of chronic disease; we discuss these in Chapter 5. In this chapter we describe several AI-enabled devices that are primarily used in data-gathering for eventual diagnosis by physicians, including cardiac monitoring, colonoscopy, teledermatology, and medically focused smartwatches. We also briefly discuss surgical robots in this chapter as a future AI-enabled medical device.

One example of a device that can gather and analyze important health data for up to 14 days is the Zio continuous cardiac monitoring device from iRhythm (similar to the device prescribed for Tony in our Preface). Compared with the clunky Holter monitors usually used now to monitor cardiac activity for 24 to 48 hours, the Zio is much less invasive and more likely to be worn for the prescribed period, as well as providing higher-quality data. The data from the monitor is uploaded to the cloud and analyzed with a variety of machine learning algorithms to detect abnormalities.

A combination of AI and miniaturization may someday revolutionize many people's least favorite routine screening procedure: the colonoscopy. In 2001 the FDA approved capsule endoscopy, a procedure where a device tiny enough to swallow can take thousands of images on its way through the digestive system—a journey that takes a few hours.

That wealth of information is astonishing, but far too much for a human observer to use without AI to do an initial screening. AI analyzes these images and flags those that might show polyps, tumors, or other anomalies. With AI's help, capsule endoscopy has become the gold standard for examining the small intestine—an area impossible to reach with conventional endoscopic approaches and also difficult to image with x-rays. The small intestine can hide ulcers, cancer, and inflammatory bowel disease, among many other conditions.

The capsule method still has to prove itself as an improvement on conventional colonoscopies, but AI is helping it get to that goal. Studies have shown that AI-enabled capsule studies can reliably detect blood in the colon, a common symptom of serious disease, and can perform better than CT scans on patients who had unsuccessful conventional colonoscopies (Mascarenhas Saraiva 2021; Deding 2020).

Permanent or semi-permanent wearable devices with health sensors are proliferating rapidly, but for the most part the data they provide has not yet been integrated with electronic health records (EHRs) or broader medical advice. Their primary value for healthcare providers is to notify healthcare professionals when emergency care is needed, such as when the Apple Watch calls for an ambulance after the wearer has a hard fall. For wearables to be useful for serious medical conditions, the healthcare industry will need a class of platforms that integrate data from multiple "medical internet of things" (MIOT) devices. They will provide both integration technologies and logic that looks at the data across devices and other sources of data. For example, a smartwatch that is measuring heart rate, blood pressure, and dehydration (by analyzing the salt content of sweat) would also need to be integrated with EHR data and weather data (to see heat and humidity) to determine if the wearer was a young adult playing tennis or a frail person with cardiac disease being overcome by heat stroke. One should generate an alarm and the other should not.

Apple is careful to say that the Apple Watch is not a medical device, but other smartwatches certainly are. Empatica's Embrace, for example, is a smartwatch specifically designed for medical monitoring that emerged from research at the MIT Media Lab. It collects medical-grade data on body temperature, blood oxygen, pulse rate, respiration, and many other standard and custom medical biomarkers. Its monitoring of electrodermal activity allows it to detect epileptic seizures and automatically notify a physician of them, and it has been approved by the FDA as a medical device for that purpose. It is also widely used in clinical trials to gather metabolic data from participants.

Surgical robots, widely used for minimally invasive procedures such as prostatectomies, hysterectomies, gall bladder removal, and heart valve repair, could someday be the ultimate AI-enabled device, but as of now the surgeon is in control at all times and no independent decisions are made by the robot. They are worth mentioning in this context, however, because autonomous surgical robots have been used successfully in academic research settings, and it is likely that they will eventually make their way into clinical practice (Haidegger 2019). When they do, they could have a major impact on how surgeries are practiced, and by whom.

Finally, AI can also be used—as it is in industrial settings on complex machinery—to predict failure of medical devices. "Predictive asset maintenance" algorithms use past failures to identify the variables that are involved in patterns of failure. In one study, for example, machine learning models were able to accurately predict the failure of defibrillators (Badnjedic 2019). As medical equipment becomes increasingly complex it is likely to benefit even more from AI-based failure prediction.

4.5   Current and future AI-enabled environments

Healthcare "environments"—both physical and virtual—are gradually evolving to include data, analytics, and AI. These environments have included exam rooms in hospitals and physicians' offices, hospital rooms and other facilities, and ambulances for urgent care. Recently they have evolved to incorporate patient portals, mobile device apps, and healthcare vans and other mobile facilities. We'll describe how AI is beginning to impact each of these settings.

Smart exam rooms. Since the widespread adoption of EHRs, patients often complain that clinicians spend most of their brief appointment staring at—or clicking or typing on—a computer screen. AI could help improve the interaction through natural language processing (NLP), in the exam room, along with prominent screens for both clinicians and patients to view.

Physicians have used NLP for years to dictate notes on patient interactions, but if properly integrated into the patient encounter, it can now also capture a patient's comments and responses, creating a complete and usually quite accurate record of a visit with a clinician, and populating the relevant parts of the patient record with updated data. These systems, sometimes referred to as Ambient Clinical Intelligence, can relieve clinicians of substantial amounts of documentation time, which often far exceed the time actually spent with patients (Ash 2019). Increasingly, NLP will also be used to call up displays and records that the clinician can discuss with a patient during the visit. Rooms with these capabilities capture the conversation between doctor and patient; NLP systems turn voice into text, and then extract key data from it. AI can also analyze video of the interaction to determine the nature of the physical exam or procedure.

AI can also mine text from past interactions to help identify and diagnose symptoms and diseases that a patient may experience well after a clinician visit. Outbound NLP that calls, emails, or texts patients can also help to drive adherence to treatments discussed and prescribed in the exam room.

Smart hospitals. Medical center construction projects are incorporating AI and robotic capabilities to reduce medical errors and improve care. At Stanford Healthcare's new $2.5 billion facility, for example, screens in rooms deliver personalized content to patients about their condition and treatments, which helps with adherence to prescribed treatment protocols (Heath 2020). Large robots in the basement of the hospital assemble individual medication packages for patients to receive via pneumatic tubes (Davenport 2021b). The operating rooms have surgical robots and AI-based analysis and recommendation systems (Whelan 2019). These smart hospitals are very expensive, but countries around the world are beginning to develop them. Japan, for example, hopes to have ten AI-enhanced hospitals in place by 2022 (Ishii 2020).

Smart ambulances. Ambulances have not historically been digitally connected to the "mothership" of the hospital or clinic, and patients have had to await arrival there to receive most treatments. That delay has led to serious health concerns for stroke victims, for example, who require rapid diagnosis and treatment. Specially equipped mobile stroke units, of which there were a few dozen worldwide in 2021 (Fassbender 2021), can dramatically improve patients' prognoses compared with conventional ambulance-based treatment (Grotta 2021), proving the potential value of mobile treatment. It's easy to see how enhanced ambulances, equipped with high bandwidth 5G mobile networks, virtual reality headsets (which use AI for some capabilities), and sensors, could provide early intervention for other conditions in addition to stroke. The NHS has already experimented with 5G-enabled ambulances and a video collaboration platform, and will roll them out across the U.K. (Palmer 2020). It seems likely that future ambulances will also make AI-based recommendations to paramedics when no physician is available through mobile networks.

Smart portals and apps. Many healthcare providers offer patient portals, typically in conjunction with their EHR. While these are useful for some purposes, they look backward and they summarize treatment through only one provider organization. Any recommendations they make are typically nonessential and nonpersonalized (in our case, for example, encouragements to get Covid-19 vaccinations long after we did so).

AI-enabled portals can potentially be more comprehensive in the data they collect and analyze (including data from wearable devices), more predictive, more recommendation-oriented, and more prioritized in their communications. Portals must become intelligent hubs that provide personalized insights. Additional functionality will provide physicians with prioritized recommendations: which patients are overdue for care and which patients' wearables or home sensors are signaling for an intervention. The Covid-19 pandemic gave a major boost to remote care via phone and video: the next step is to consolidate those gains by integrating those encounters into smart portals.

There are examples of this type of portal in Asia. For example, the Ping An Good Doctor system is the largest mobile medical application in the world, with more than 72.6 million active users and more than 373 million registered users in China. A proprietary AI-based medical software platform supports an in-house medical team of more than 1,800 doctors and related health professionals to provide 24/7 medical services to users through online consultations (an average of more than 830,000 per day), referrals, registrations, and online drug purchases and delivery arrangements. The company's stated objective is to provide every family in China with a family doctor, every person with a health-related e-profile, and everyone with a healthcare management plan through "mobile medical + AI technology." A similar Good Doctor system is available in Southeast Asia through a joint venture between Ping An, Japan's Softbank, and the Southeast Asian "super-app" startup Grab (Davenport 2021a).

If the drugs, devices, and facilities we describe in this chapter become available, successful healthcare will depend on how much patients engage with them, how much provider and payer organizations attend to whether they engage, and (most importantly) what happens to their health as a result—topics we address in the next chapter.

References

Ash, M., et al. (2019). How AI in the exam room could reduce physician burnout. *Harvard Business Review*, November 12. https://hbr.org/2019/11/how-ai-in-the-exam-room-could-reduce-physician-burnout.

Badnjedic, A., et al. (2019). Evidence-based clinical engineering: machine learning algorithms for prediction of defibrillator performance. *Biomedical Signal Processing and Control*, 54: 101629. https://www.sciencedirect.com/science/article/abs/pii/S1746809419302101?dgcid=coauthr

BioNTech and InstaDeep (2020). BioNTech and InstaDeep announce strategic collaboration and form AI innovation lab to develop novel immunotherapies. Press release, November 25. https://investors.biontech.de/node/8806/pdf.

Davenport, T. (2021a). The future of work now: Good Doctor technology for intelligent telemedicine in Southeast Asia. *Forbes*, March 2. https://www.forbes.com/sites/tomdavenport/2021/03/02/the-future-of-work-now-good-doctor-technology-for-intelligent-telemedicine-in-southeast-asia/?sh=3155948a5289.

Davenport, T. (2021b). The future of work now: pharmacists and the robotic pharmacy at Stanford Health Care. *Forbes*, January 18. https://www.forbes.com/sites/tomdavenport/2021/01/18/the-future-of-work-now-pharmacists-and-the-robotic-pharmacy-at-stanford-health-care/?sh=3b1c53093937.

Deding, U., Herp, J., Havshoei, A.L., et al. (2020). Colon capsule endoscopy versus CT colonography after incomplete colonoscopy: application of artificial intelligence algorithms to identify complete colonic investigations. *United European Gastroenterology Journal*, 8(7): 782–9. http://doi.org/10.1177/2050640620937593.

Fassbender, K., Merzou, F., Lesmeister, M., et al. (2021). Impact of mobile stroke units. *Journal of Neurology, Neurosurgery & Psychiatry*, 92(8): 815–22. http://doi.org/10.1136/jnnp-2020-324005.

Foundation Medicine (2020). Foundation Medicine receives FDA approval for FoundationOne®CDx as the companion diagnostic for LYNPARZA® to identify patients with HRR-mutated metastatic castration-resistant prostate cancer. Press release, May 20. https://www.foundationmedicine.com/press-releases/d6fffcbf-08ff-45b6-9e4a-9f69536c32ce.

Freedman, D.H. (2019). Hunting for new drugs with AI. *Nature*, 576(7787): S49–S53. http://doi.org/10.1038/d41586-019-03846-0.

Grotta, J.C., Yamal, J.M., Parker, S.A., et al. (2021). Prospective, multicenter, controlled trial of mobile stroke units. *New England Journal of Medicine*, 385(11): 971–81. http://doi.org/10.1056/NEJMoa2103879.

Haidegger, T. (2019). Autonomy for surgical robots: concepts and paradigms. *IEEE Transactions on Medical Robotics and Bionics*, 1(2): 65–76. http://doi.org/ 10.1109/TMRB.2019.2913282.

Heath, S. (2020). Smart hospitals making the future of patient experience a reality. *PatientEngagementHIT*,   January   24.   https://patientengagementhit.com/ features/smart-hospitals-making-the-future-of-patient-experience-a-reality.

Ishii, E., Ebner, D.K., Kimura, S., Agha-Mir-Salim, L., Uchimido, R. and Celi, L.A. (2020). The advent of medical artificial intelligence: lessons from the Japanese approach. *Journal of Intensive Care Medicine*, 8: 35. http://doi.org/10.1186/ s40560-020-00452-5.

Kahn, J. (2020). Know when to fold 'em: how a company best known for playing games used A.I. to solve one of biology's greatest mysteries. *Fortune*, November   30.   https://fortune.com/2020/11/30/deepmind-solved-protein -folding-alphafold/.

Mascarenhas Saraiva, M., Ferreira, J.P.S., Cardoso, H., et al. (2021). Artificial intelligence and colon capsule endoscopy: automatic detection of blood in colon capsule endoscopy using a convolutional neural network. *Endoscopy International Open*, 9(8): E1264–E1268. http://doi.org/10.1055/a-1490-8960.

MIT Sloan Management Review (2021). Me, myself and AI podcast. Dave Johnson, Moderna Chief Data and AI Officer, July 13. https://sloanreview.mit .edu/audio/ai-and-the-covid-19-vaccine-modernas-dave-johnson/.

Palmer, M. (2020). Smart ambulances and wearables offer route to speedier treatments. *Financial Times*, November 24. https://www.ft.com/content/35210279 -1361-4cab-b179-a725eb6731d8.

Whelan, K. (2019). Artificial intelligence in the operating room. *Medical Expo*, July 1. https://emag.medicalexpo.com/real-time-artificial-intelligence-system -for-the-operating-room/.

5   AI for engaging patients and improving health

5.1   Introduction

We've discussed AI's vast potential for diagnosing and treating disease, but its potential for prevention, and for management of chronic disease, may be even greater. In this chapter we'll look at how patients might have their glucose levels or erratic heartbeats managed by smart devices, use their smartphones to identify potentially cancerous skin lesions, be nudged into healthier behavior by AI-enabled reminders, or improve their emotional health by downloading their troubles to an AI-based therapist. In this chapter we focus on AI and intelligent devices for general health management and chronic conditions, precision behavioral "nudges," and AI for population health.

Some medical devices can be used for acute care, management of chronic disease, or overall health monitoring. The Apple Watch can call an ambulance when necessary for an acute health condition. It can measure heart rate, sleep quality, blood oxygen, and all kinds of activity—from distance biked to the speed of a tennis serve to the number of waves caught by a surfer. It can detect when the wearer has had a hard fall. It can take an electrocardiogram from the wearer's finger resting on the watch face. No wonder it has the tagline: "The future of health is on your wrist."

The future of health may end up on all our wrists, but the present of health is still all around us—and sometimes difficult to assemble. We'll look at some of the issues surrounding the AI-enabled personal health ecosystem, including surmounting possible regulatory hurdles and addressing threats to users' privacy.

5.2   The dermatologist is in: image analysis of suspicious lesions

Skin cancer is the most common of cancers, and frequently missed because most people don't see a dermatologist regularly and primary care providers may not have the expertise to identify a problem and send the patient to a specialist to follow up. Some patients can't be bothered to see a doctor about each new skin eruption and don't discover life-threatening cancers until it's too late. Others obsess over every tiny bump, looking through images online and fretting about whether their growth is a match for something deadly. Neither group has had a simple and reliable way to monitor how their skin changes over time, even though those changes can signal cancer.

An AI algorithm trained on a large library of skin images can flag possible problems quickly and cheaply, helping propel the heedless group to the dermatologist when necessary and easing the anxieties of the worried well. Google is working with Stanford University physicians on just such an application, trained to distinguish potentially dangerous lesions based on three smartphone photos (Bui 2021).

Google is hardly alone on the track of AI-enabled dermatology imaging for patients. Miiskin, based in Denmark, claims to be the first AI-enabled dermatology app, and in addition to its basic consumer app has a "pro" version for dermatologists to use with their patients. Patients upload photos to the company's cloud, where the AI notes any concerning features. Photos taken over time allow the app to track growths and flag changes. The goal is not to determine whether a skin lesion is cancerous, but simply whether it has changed and/or looks suspicious enough for the patient to visit a dermatologist. Hundreds of thousands of patients have uploaded images to the Miiskin cloud, and the app is included in the U.K. National Health Service's app library (Davenport 2020).

5.3   The "artificial pancreas": closed loop insulin pumps

Around 38 million people worldwide live with insulin-dependent (Type 1) diabetes. Their lives depend on administering the correct amount of insulin to keep their blood glucose stable. Eating, drinking, and exercise can all change the amount that's correct. A drop in blood sugar while they're asleep or not paying attention can cause life-threatening hypoglycemia.

Automatically tracking blood glucose levels and administering insulin accordingly is a task well suited for AI, and several manufacturers have introduced "closed loop" insulin pumps that combine glucose sensors and continuous insulin pumps with an algorithm that allows them to communicate. After a week or so of training to learn the user's patterns of insulin use, the algorithm can handle automatic mode, where the pump responds to information supplied by the sensor. The patient may have to approve a dose if the sensor recommends an amount that falls outside the patient's usual pattern. These devices are the closest that technology has come to duplicating the functions of a healthy pancreas.

The software can also collect information from the pump and sensor so users and their physicians can track the numbers and look at trends. User data can also help manufacturers refine their algorithms and make these devices smarter over time. Studies have already shown an advantage for the closed-loop system over other methods of insulin delivery (McAuley 2022; Brown 2019), and the technology also holds promise for Type 2 diabetes, a much more widespread condition (Boughton 2021).

5.4   Smarter pacemakers: customized nudging and remote monitoring through AI

The first implantable cardiac devices to regulate heartbeat were a lifesaving technology, but often a shocking one—literally. They delivered an electrical pulse to reset a patient's heart rhythm, often powerful enough for the patient to feel. The quest to make them less invasive and more effective—in other words, smarter—has been continuous. In the past decade, remote monitoring began allowing patients to have their devices recalibrated as changes were needed, rather than every few months when they visited their cardiologist. A recent development is Bluetooth-based smartphone monitoring, which replaces specialized transmission consoles that don't always connect successfully with the provider. The app connected patients successfully with their providers 94 percent of the time in a recent study, compared with 77–87 percent using earlier types of wireless transmission (Tarakji 2021).

The most advanced implanted pacemakers and defibrillators use AI for calibration. The algorithms are based on electrical impulse data from the hearts of thousands of patients and can more accurately predict what the heart will do and how to nudge it back to a regular heartbeat.

The next step? Perhaps "bionic neurons"—artificial nerve cells that help the pacemaker adapt more naturally to changes in the body's demands on the heart (between running and walking, for example) by receiving and transmitting electrical signals related to blood pressure and oxygen levels. These smart chips have already been tested successfully in the U.K. in animals through CResPace, a project funded by the European Union (Cordis 2021).

5.5   Battling chronic kidney disease: ClosedLoop.ai

The Centers for Medicare and Medicaid Services (CMS), the U.S. agency responsible for federally funded healthcare, recently held a contest for inventing new ways to improve health outcomes using artificial intelligence. It drew more than 300 entries. The winner, ClosedLoop.ai, tackled one of the most expensive and unmanageable health problems of all: chronic kidney disease (CKD). The $1.6 million prize was a prelude to the $34 million in fresh venture funding that the company received a few months after its win (Landi 2021).

Medicare spends billions of dollars—more than a quarter of its annual patient care budget— treating CKD and its complications. ClosedLoop's solution starts with prevention and early intervention. Its algorithms analyze data from electronic health records and medical and pharmacy claims to monitor key changes, identify patients at risk for CKD because of diabetes or other health problems, and anticipate and avoid specific adverse impacts. Patients can be monitored for signs of failing kidneys and for how well they adhere to their medication regimens. For patients who already have CKD, the algorithm can anticipate their risk of particular complications and the chances that they'll develop hospital-associated complications—for example, sepsis or kidney injury. The AI also reminds physicians to choose medications for CKD patients that are not toxic to the kidneys, and monitor them closely when there's no choice (CMS 2021).

5.6   AI for mental health

When many people think about applying AI to mental health, the chatbot therapist may be the first idea that springs to mind. While this type of therapy has shown some promise in very specific contexts (see below), it's far from the only way that AI can help.

"The new technological capabilities of smartphones, artificial intelligence, social media and virtual reality are already changing mental healthcare in unforeseen and exciting ways," concluded an international panel of experts in a comprehensive review paper in the journal *World Psychiatry* (Torous 2021, 318).

They identified a range of applications that helped with eating disorders, substance abuse, depression, and anxiety, and predicted an increase in personalized digital mental healthcare from a combination of AI and sensor technology known as just-in-time adaptive intervention (JITAI). For example, a wearable device like the smartwatch described at the beginning of the chapter knows the wearer's location, and vital signs like blood pressure, temperature, or pulse. The wearer could choose to teach the device to identify when they are anxious or depressed and make different recommendations depending on whether the wearer is out at a club or at home in bed.

Applications can predict mental health crises just by tracking changes in mobility patterns and smartphone use, as long as patients keep the app active on their phone. For example, 17 patients with schizophrenia in active treatment at a state mental health clinic in Boston used such an app for up to three months. The rate of behavioral anomalies detected in the two weeks prior to a relapse was 71 percent higher than the rate of anomalies during other time periods. Real-time detection of these kinds of behavioral anomalies could signal the need for an intervention before an escalation of symptoms and relapse occur, reducing patient suffering and reducing the cost of care (Barnett 2018).

5.6.1   Therapy by app

Is downloading your troubles onto an AI — trained to deliver responses that sound like therapy—as effective as talking to a human therapist? An app called Woebot walks users through a series of questions that require no more than a word or two to answer, hoping to zero in on what's bothering them and suggest coping strategies. It offers a specific therapeutic technique called cognitive behavior therapy (CBT), also very widely used by human therapists to treat depression and other common mental health conditions. CBT is well suited as a training ground for AI therapists because it's designed to address and change specific feelings and behaviors, rather than to be a free-ranging exploration of the patient's mental health issues and experiences.

In a study of 70 young adults over two weeks, half had up to 20 sessions with Woebot and the other half was given an e-book on depression in college students. Tested for depression and anxiety both before and after, the Woebot group experienced significantly greater relief from depression (although both groups reported about the same reduction in anxiety) (Fitzpatrick 2017).

5.6.2   Potential pitfalls

Mental health services have always been plagued by the dangers of misdiagnosis and provider bias against patients. While AI-enabled mental health applications can allay some of those difficulties by removing humans from the interaction, they still have been created by humans and can carry the imperfections of their creators. For example, an AI-based application called NarxCare is widely used in the U.S.A. to flag patterns of opioid abuse and help providers identify and block patients who may be "doctor-shopping" for painkiller prescriptions. An article in *Wired* magazine described the plight of a woman mistakenly flagged as a possible addict by the algorithm because of painkillers prescribed in her name for her pets. The algorithm didn't understand that they were veterinary versions, and the woman spent months unraveling the mix-up so that she could escape providers' assumptions that she was an abuser of opioids and regain access to the pain medications she used for endometriosis. The maker of the application denied that such mix-ups were common, but social media groups were filled with tales of patients who'd been flagged in error (Szalavitz 2021).

5.7   AI and precision nudging

"Nudge theory," a concept in behavioral economics, gained prominence with the 2008 book *Nudge: Improving Decisions about Health, Wealth, and Happiness* by Nobel prize-winning economist Richard Thaler and legal scholar Cass Sunstein of Harvard. The basic idea is to make it easier for people to make better decisions—for example, by putting healthier choices at eye level in the grocery store and making junk food less visible or harder to reach, or by setting up workplace savings plans as "opt-out," rather than "opt-in," so that people must actively choose *not* to save. A related concept is "choice architecture," which structures the available choices to move the chooser toward the architect's desired result (Thaler 2008).

Penn Medicine, at the University of Pennsylvania in Philadelphia, has created a "nudge unit" to investigate how nudges and changes in choice architecture can influence the behavior of both physicians and patients. For example, one of the unit's projects studied several ways to structure financial incentives to encourage obese Penn employees to increase their exercise levels. A loss-framed incentive, in which money was placed in a virtual account and taken away if goals were not achieved, was the most effective—relative to the control group, physical activity goal achievement increased by 50 percent. A gain-framed incentive, which rewarded participants after goals were achieved, was no different from the control arm (Patel 2016).

In another study, "gamification"—turning the achievement of daily exercise goals into a competition among families—substantially increased exercise among the gamers compared with a control group, and the gaming group maintained an increased activity level even after the study was over (Patel 2017).

It's easy to see how AI could individualize these subtle influences on behavior, by adjusting goals or incentives based on the user's health profile, and by identifying ways to enable the desired actions. A smart app could suggest new routes for a walking routine, or coach users to step up their exertion level, monitoring their heart rate and rewarding them when they do.

In a "wired" grocery store, an app could steer its user to foods and ingredients suitable for specialized diets or specific healthy eating goals, and propose recipes based on the day's specials or the available produce. Kroger, for example, already provides "Wellness Your Way" recommendations for healthy foods and recipes. More sophisticated AI systems could automatically "referee" a fitness challenge with multiple participants.

A startup, Well, creates personalized nudges for its members using AI. It makes highly tailored clinical recommendations, and it even calculates the level of rewards for good behavior based on historical adherence to medications and treatments. Those who are less adherent get higher rewards in order to change their behavior. It has nudge-related content for over 20 different medical conditions, including hypertension and diabetes.

Several insurance companies, including Manulife and John Hancock in North America, and AIA and Ping An in Asia, have partnered with the U.K. firm Vitality to use smartwatches to monitor physical activity and other wellness behaviors of their policyholders. Like Well, they offer recommendations to avoid or treat chronic health conditions, though the recommendations are less personalized and clinically based.

5.8   AI for population health

For providers, some of the most promising AI applications are those that can help them manage and improve health across patient populations: flagging people who are at risk and getting them the help they need before they develop chronic health problems. Trained on large databases of patients with known health outcomes, AI can review years' worth of patient data and spot the warning signs of diabetes from trends in lab tests, or find patients whose family histories may reveal elevated risks for heritable diseases. A vigilant primary care physician might do the same for individual patients, but AI can be vigilant for everyone.

Geisinger Health System, a Pennsylvania-based provider that also acts as health insurer for many of its patients, has pioneered many innovative uses of information technology (including offering genomic screening and counseling as part of routine care, one of the first health systems to do so in the U.S.A.). Geisinger is using AI to find patients in its population who are overdue for colonoscopies and are also at increased risk for colorectal cancer, based on the results of routine blood tests already on file. Its application of this technology was awarded second place in CMS's AI Health Outcomes Challenge (CMS 2021).

5.9   Adoption issues

As noted at the beginning of the chapter, AI-enabled health monitoring and nudging are already here and will continue to expand rapidly in both quantity of data collected and variety of applications. The fundamental questions for healthcare executives are: What role will their organizations play in this new health information ecosystem? Are they ready to leverage this new resource to help patients? How much control can they expect to maintain?

While it's unlikely that AI-based health apps will "disintermediate" hospitals and clinics to the same degree that, for example, online booking did to travel agents, they will almost certainly empower many patients to become more engaged in their own care and to expect a higher level of responsiveness and partnership from their healthcare providers. If their existing providers aren't ready, they may welcome overtures from those who have made it a priority to integrate digital capabilities into their relationship with patients.

As with any transformative technology, the road to full implementation is likely to be twisty and filled with obstacles. As AI becomes an important element in applications to maintain health, manage disease, and monitor populations, several barriers or speed bumps will come into play.

5.9.1   Regulatory considerations

Purveyors of health-related consumer applications have largely eluded regulation so far. The U.S. Food and Drug Administration (FDA) distinguishes between health and medical apps, which it includes in its regulatory framework, and "wellness" apps, which are unregulated in much the way food supplements are, as long as they stay away from making any claims about their power to treat disease or improve health. The European Union draws a similar distinction.

However, as AI-enabled apps become more sophisticated, seek to prove that they have an impact on health, and generate more information used by patients and providers to make treatment decisions, they will come to look more like medical devices and be regulated accordingly. We discuss the overall regulation of healthcare AI elsewhere, but consumer apps face some specific issues of their own.

In the U.S.A., the Federal Trade Commission (FTC) has developed specific guidance for mobile health app developers that recognizes the implications of these apps across multiple regulatory areas: not just the FDA, but the FTC itself, which prohibits deceptive commercial practices, and the Health Insurance Portability and Accountability Act (HIPAA), which governs the protection and sharing of protected personal health information and requires reporting of breaches of patient privacy (FTC 2016).

AI will not always work as billed, and when a health-related AI application fails, it can be life-threatening. The marketers of two app-supported smartphone accessories, which claimed to analyze the user's breath and measure blood alcohol content (BAC) accurately enough to determine whether it was safe to drive home after a night out, agreed in 2017 to settle FTC charges that they lacked scientific evidence to back up their advertising claims. Breathometer, Inc. had to notify all its customers of the charges and pay them full refunds, and the company and its founder were barred from making any such claims in the future unless they're supported by rigorous testing. At this writing the company still has a website but its only advertised product is a device that measures the quality of the user's oral hygiene, and its terms and conditions include extensive disclaimers (FTC 2017).

5.9.2   Building patient trust

Cheerleaders for incorporating AI into routine healthcare sometimes fail to recognize its potentially negative aspects for privacy-conscious consumers. Patients will have an increasingly lopsided relationship with health and medical AI, which will understand more about them than they understand about it.

The U.S. National Academy of Medicine recently published a comprehensive review: *Artificial Intelligence in Healthcare: The Hope, The Hype, The Promise, The Peril*. It contained this summation of what the industry must do to maintain patients' privacy while still reaping the benefits of using AI:

> In general, there is tension between privacy-protecting approaches and access to big data for the development, validation, and oversight of health care AI. For instance, Google was sued for privacy violations in 2019 as a result of an agreement with the University of Chicago Medical Center to use the system's data in AI and other big data applications (Cohen 2019). Higher protections for patient data, whether regarding front-end collection or back-end use, increase the hurdles for the development of health care AI (Ford 2016) ... However, privacy and innovation in health care AI are not in strict opposition. Newer technological approaches such as differential privacy (Malin 2013) and dynamic consent (Kaye 2015) can help enable development while still protecting privacy. In fact, the desire to protect privacy can be its own spur to the development of innovative technologies to collect, manage, and use health data ... [I]t will demand careful policymaking and continued engagement by stakeholders at various levels. (Matheny 2019, 206)

It seems certain that AI-enabled routine health monitoring and care will fundamentally change the relationship between patients and their providers, whether patients buy the technology for themselves or have it prescribed for them by providers trying to help them manage their health. It's too early to predict all the ramifications of this trend for healthcare providers, but not too early to start paying close attention.

References

Barnett, I., Torous, J., Staples, P., Sandoval, L., Keshavan, M. and Onnela, J.P. (2018). Relapse prediction in schizophrenia through digital phenotyping: a pilot study. *Neuropsychopharmacology*, 43(8): 1660–66. http://doi.org/10.1038/s41386-018-0030-z.

Boughton, C.K., Tripyla, A., Hartnell, S., et al. (2021). Fully automated closed-loop glucose control compared with standard insulin therapy in adults with type 2 diabetes requiring dialysis: an open-label, randomized crossover trial. *Nature Medicine*, 27(8): 1471–6. http://doi.org/10.1038/s41591-021-01453-z [published correction appears in *Nature Medicine*, 27(10): 1850].

Brown, S.A., Kovatchev, B.P., Raghinaru, D., et al. (2019). Six-month randomized, multicenter trial of closed-loop control in type 1 diabetes. *New England Journal of Medicine*, 381(18): 1707–17. http://doi.org/10.1056/NEJMoa1907863.

Bui, P. (2021). Using AI to help find answers to common skin conditions. Google/The Keyword/Health, May 18. https://blog.google/technology/health/ai-dermatology-preview-io-2021/.

CMS (2021). CMS selects winner and runner-up in artificial intelligence health outcomes challenge. Press release, April 30. https://www.cms.gov/newsroom/press-releases/cms-selects-winner-and-runner-artificial-intelligence-health-outcomes-challenge.

Cohen, I.G. and Mello, M.M. (2019). Big data, big tech, and protecting patient privacy. *JAMA*, 322(12): 1141–2. http://doi.org/10.1001/jama.2019.11365.

Cordis (2021). A smart pacemaker to prevent heart failure and revolutionise bioelectronic implants. EU Research Results. Press release, June 16. https://cordis.europa.eu/article/id/430268-a-smart-pacemaker-to-prevent-heart-failure-and-revolutionise-bioelectronic-implants.

Davenport, T. (2020). The future of work now: AI-assisted skin imaging. *Forbes.com*, November 3. https://www.forbes.com/sites/tomdavenport/2020/11/03/the-future-of-work-now-ai-assisted-skin-imaging/?sh=396188827e40.

Federal Trade Commission (FTC) (2016). Mobile health apps interactive tool. April. https://www.ftc.gov/tips-advice/business-center/guidance/mobile-health-apps-interactive-tool.

Federal Trade Commission (FTC) (2017). 'Breathometer' marketers settle FTC charges of misrepresenting ability to accurately measure users' blood alcohol content. Press release, January 23. https://www.ftc.gov/news-events/press-releases/2017/01/breathometer-marketers-settle-ftc-charges-misrepresenting-ability.

Fitzpatrick, K.K., Darcy, A. and Vierhile, M. (2017). Delivering cognitive behavior therapy to young adults with symptoms of depression and anxiety using a fully automated conversational agent (Woebot): a randomized controlled trial. *JMIR Mental Health*, 4(2): e19. http://doi.org/10.2196/mental.7785.

Ford, R. and Price, W. (2016). Privacy and accountability in black-box medicine. *Michigan Telecommunications and Technology Law Review*, 23: 1–43.

Kaye, J., Whitley, E.A., Lund, D., Morrison, M., Teare, H., and Melham, K. (2015). Dynamic consent: a patient interface for twenty-first-century research networks. *European Journal of Human Genetics*, 23(2): 141–6. http://doi.org/10.1038/ejhg.2014.71.

Landi, H. (2021). Fresh off its win in the CMS Challenge, ClosedLoop.ai nabs $34M to build out 'explainable' AI. *Fierce Healthcare*, August 18. https://www.fiercehealthcare.com/tech/fresh-off-its-win-cms-challenge-closedloop-ai-nabs-34m-to-build-out-explainable-ai.

Malin, B.A., Emam, K.E. and O'Keefe, C.M. (2013). Biomedical data privacy: problems, perspectives, and recent advances. *Journal of the American Medical Informatics Association*, 20(1): 2–6. http://doi.org/:10.1136/amiajnl-2012-001509.

Matheny, M., Israni, S., Ahmed, M. and Whicher, D. (2019). *Artificial Intelligence in Health Care: The Hope, the Hype, the Promise, the Peril.* NAM Special Publication. Washington, D.C.: National Academy of Medicine.

McAuley, S.A., Trawley, S., Vogrin, S., et al. (2022). Closed-loop insulin delivery versus sensor-augmented pump therapy in older adults with type 1 diabetes

(ORACL): a randomized, crossover trial. *Diabetes Care*, 45(2): 381–90. https://doi.org/10.2337/dc21-1667.

Patel, M.S., Benjamin, E.J., Volpp, K.G., et al. (2017). Effect of a game-based intervention designed to enhance social incentives to increase physical activity among families: the BE FIT randomized clinical trial. *JAMA Internal Medicine*, 177(11): 1586–93. http://doi.org/10.1001/jamainternmed.2017.3458.

Patel, M.S., Volpp, K.G., Rosin, R., et al. (2016). A randomized trial of social comparison feedback and financial incentives to increase physical activity. *American Journal of Health Promotion*, 30(6): 416–24. http://doi.org/10.1177/0890117116658195.

Szalavitz, M. (2021). The pain was unbearable. So why did doctors turn her away? *Wired*, August 11. https://www.wired.com/story/opioid-drug-addiction-algorithm-chronic-pain/.

Tarakji, K.G., Zaidi, A.M., Zweibel, S.L., et al. (2021). Performance of first pacemaker to use smart device app for remote monitoring. *Heart Rhythm O2*, 2(5): 463–71. http://doi.org/10.1016/j.hroo.2021.07.008; https://www.heartrhythmopen.com/article/S2666-5018(21)00125-2/fulltext.

Thaler RH, Sunstein CR. (2008). *Nudge: Improving Decisions about Health, Wealth, and Happiness*. Yale University Press, New Haven, CT.

Torous, J., Bucci, S., Bell, I.H., et al. (2021). The growing field of digital psychiatry: current evidence and the future of apps, social media, chatbots, and virtual reality. *World Psychiatry*, 20(3): 318–35. http://doi.org/10.1002/wps.20883.

6   Administering and paying for healthcare with AI

6.1   Introduction

Most of the sex appeal of healthcare AI is on the clinical side. It's exciting to consider the potential benefits from AI curing cancer, warding off diabetes, predicting when grandma is likely to fall and break her hip, or helping people improve their overall health.

Unfortunately, the full realization of these applications is in the future. The good news for anyone involved in healthcare administration? Much less sexy applications—improving payment processes, limiting fraud, or schedule operating rooms more efficiently—are here now. Better and less expensive healthcare administration through AI is currently in reach. Anyone involved in providing healthcare should seriously consider investing in AI for this purpose. It may not lend itself to flashy press releases, but its quiet ability to make things run more smoothly and efficiently may earn the gratitude of everyone who works for, or uses, a healthcare system.

6.2   The case for administrative AI

Everyone would like to reduce the cost of healthcare, and administrative costs are a natural target because reducing them doesn't require cutting the cost, quality, or availability of clinical care. While this interest is most intense in the U.S.A., which spends more per capita on healthcare than any other country, there is room for administrative cost reductions almost everywhere. One recent comparison suggests that administrative costs take up $2,500 per person in the U.S.A. per year, and $550 in Canada— with the U.K. and European countries in between these two extremes (Himmelstein 2020). As a percentage of healthcare spending, administrative costs are 34 percent of U.S. spending and only 17 percent in Canada. But even Canada may be able to trim its administrative costs.

Healthcare economists in the U.S.A. often argue that reducing administrative costs is one of the most feasible ways to cut overall costs for healthcare. David Cutler, a Harvard economist who was one of the architects of the Affordable Care Act, has proposed a series of changes to administrative processes that he argues could save $50 billion in costs (Cutler 2020). Some of these proposals hinge on AI, such as an automated claims clearinghouse and automated prior authorization processes.

Administrative processes are a tempting target for AI adoption because they aren't subject to regulatory approval. Clinical AI programs, as we have pointed out, must prove their safety and efficacy to regulators. No government signoff is needed for a better way to process prior authorizations or to get patients to pay what they owe. When the government is the payer, relevant administrative applications have to comply with its prescribed processes, but for internal administration, providers are free to employ AI in any way that benefits them.

Many provider institutions—particularly in the U.S.A. but in other countries as well—are seeking ways to apply AI for administrative purposes. They work directly with payers, for example, to smooth and speed claims or prior authorization processes. They look for ways to identify patients who need help paying their medical bills—sometimes even in advance of incurring them. They use AI to ensure proper disease coding on bills, or to make appointment scheduling easier for patients. We'll describe each of these applications and more in greater detail in this chapter.

6.3   The revenue cycle and AI

(*Note: Because of the high administrative costs of U.S. healthcare and the peculiarities of its healthcare financing system, the discussion in this section is U.S.-centric. Readers from other countries may identify certain aspects that are applicable to their national systems.)*

In the U.S.A., payer/provider interactions about claims and reimbursements are very extensive, and are known as the "revenue cycle." Historically, payers and providers have not always been on the same page. Providers try to maximize their reimbursements, and payers try to minimize them. Providers resent any interventions by payers in the care process, and payers often block payment for care that they deem unnecessary.

Increasingly, however, providers and payers seem to be, if not on the same page, at least reading the same book. Both are interested in—or at least reconciled to—moving away from fee-for-service care, and toward value-based care. Both want to reduce administrative costs. Both believe that AI can help in the process.

Administrative "pain points" in revenue cycle processes include:

• estimates of out-of-pocket costs for patients
• coding of diseases and treatments
• prior authorizations
• claims status checking
• fraud, waste, and abuse detection.

They are being addressed with AI solutions by providers, payers, and third-party solution providers. The question is not whether AI can help with these issues, but whose system will prevail and whether AI applications will end up being redundant or overlapping.

6.3.1   Estimating out-of-pocket costs

It can be difficult to determine in advance what a patient will have to pay for treatment, particularly for a complex medical intervention in a large hospital system. Many hospital systems don't have a clear itemization of their costs, there's no consistent process for determining what insurance coverage is available ahead of time, and the patient's out-of-pocket costs may vary depending on whether they have "met their deductible" for the year. (One patient's health plan may require them to pay thousands out of pocket every year before full insurance coverage starts, while another's may require no deductible at all.)

Machine learning can help sort it all out, based on what similar patients have paid at the hospital in the past. Baylor Scott & White Health (BSWHealth), a provider system in Texas that runs 52 hospitals, uses healthcare AI vendor Waystar's automated price estimation tool to give every patient an estimate of their full costs before they receive care. The tool pulls real-time eligibility and benefit data from the patient's insurer, as well as how much is left in their deductible. Charges and contracted rates are also loaded in.

BSWHealth employees used to generate estimates by hand using different spreadsheets and fee schedules. The tool allows 70 percent of estimates to be calculated without human intervention, and it refines its algorithm continuously by comparing its estimates with each patient's actual bill.

Sarah Knodel, the Senior VP of Revenue Cycle, says BSWHealth has heard positive feedback from patients over the eight years it's been using the tool. The system's financial counselors can use the estimates to discuss options for payment in advance of care, and BSW Health has seen improvements of 60–100 percent on advance payments, depending on the therapeutic area. Physicians are also happy with estimates in advance because patients are much less likely to cancel scheduled procedures when they're confident about what their bill will be.

Knodel decided that the estimates should be made available to patients so that they could do price comparisons across medical providers in advance of receiving care. In addition to being extremely patient-friendly, this policy allowed BSWHealth to be compliant with new U.S. government healthcare price transparency rules that went into effect in 2021. Many providers have struggled with the requirements, and at this writing compliance has lagged (Ellerbeck 2021).

6.3.2 Coding of diseases and treatments

Since the seventeenth century in England, diseases and causes of death have been classified—originally for statistical analysis of causes of death in the London Bills of Mortality. The first attempt to create an international categorization scheme was in 1893 with the International List of Causes of Death, compiled by the International Statistical Institute. That list has evolved into the International Classification of Disease (ICD), which is maintained and updated by the World Health Organization (WHO). It includes codes not only for diseases and causes of injury, but also for treatments. Because our understanding of disease has deepened and treatments keep proliferating, the ICD system has become increasingly complex with every revision. ICD-11, the most recent iteration of the system as of this writing, has 55,000 different global codes (up from 14,000 in ICD-10), and individual countries often add more depending on how they use the system.

ICD codes play a vital role in measuring health around the world. When Covid-19 was identified, for example, the WHO assigned it ICD-10 code U07.1, and that code was one important way to track cases and deaths from the virus.

ICD codes are widely used globally for reimbursement as well. The U.S.A., for example, expanded ICD-10 by a factor of 10 (70,000 codes for diseases and another 70,000 for treatments) to make it precise enough for medical billing, and we expect it to aggressively expand ICD-11 as well. (To further complicate matters, the U.S.A. also uses the Current Procedural Terminology, or CPT, coding system, developed by the American Medical Association, for physician services.)

Where ICD codes are used for billing, the provider's revenue flow depends on accurate and complete coding. But given the complexity of coding systems, it is virtually impossible for even the best human coder to translate a diagnosis into the relevant codes without external help. It's not just a matter of finding the right code: there is often more than one way to code a diagnosis or treatment, and the medical coder has to decide on the most appropriate choices.

As a result, many providers (or their coding services vendors) use natural language processing AI to analyze clinical documentation (charts and notes) and provide a preliminary coding. Human coders check the machine's coding approach in almost every case, but the combination of human and machine coding is generally much faster than human coding alone. As coding becomes even more complex—and it always becomes more complex over time—we expect that AI-based coding will become even more prevalent, and that the human role in reviewing codes will diminish.

6.3.3   Prior authorization

Prior authorization is the process of seeking approval for a patient's treatment from the payer before that treatment is supplied. It is probably most burdensome in complex private payer situations like those in the U.S.A., but virtually every country requires some prior authorization for specialized care even when the government is the only payer.

In a 2020 survey of 1,000 physicians by the American Medical Association, respondents complained not only about administrative time and cost from prior authorization, but also about how it causes problems in patient care (AMA 2021). On average, physicians and their staff spent two days per week seeking prior authorizations, 94 percent reported care delays because of authorization problems, and 79 percent said that prior authorization sometimes led patients to abandon treatment. One in three reported that prior authorization had led to a serious adverse event for their patients.

Both providers and payers are interested in using AI to help with prior authorizations. In fact, it was the first commercial project for IBM Watson back in 2013, in cooperation with the insurer Wellpoint (now Anthem). Though Watson didn't prove to be well suited to automating prior authorization, Anthem, and many other payers, as well as multiple AI startups, are still pursuing it.

United Healthcare, the largest commercial payer in the U.S.A., has a working pilot. Mitch Morris, until recently head of Optum Insight—a business unit of United that focuses on AI and analytics projects—said the company is trying to create a "frictionless revenue cycle" that automates most prior authorizations. The goal is to initiate an authorization when a physician is entering an order into an electronic medical records system. A real-time interface to the payer's claim system results in an immediate automated review and approval if the order meets the payer's criteria. "We want to approve the right treatment, the first time," Morris said.

If the order doesn't fulfill the criteria for approval, the system prompts the physician for more or different information. For example, an authorization for an MRI for back pain requires the patient to have had three months of pain that has not responded to medication. If the criteria are met, the physician automatically gets an authorization code. Morris said that insurance companies eventually approve authorization requests 85 percent of the time anyway, so why not automate the process? He acknowledged that doctors and patients hate the current process, which he called a "denials dance."

Optum Insight has piloted the automated approval system at a cancer center it owns in Nevada. Chemotherapy is approved instantly 65 percent of the time.

Provider organizations are also pursuing solutions to the prior authorization problem. Yale New Haven Health is working with a vendor called Olive. Using robotic process automation (RPA), the system reviews orders entered into the electronic medical record (EMR). Using machine learning (ML), the system recommends changes to the order, based on past denials that the hospital has received, to improve its chances of approval. The head of patient financial services at Yale New Haven says the system has sped up the resolution of claims and receipt of cash (LaPointe 2020). Another Olive user, Watertown Regional Health Center in Wisconsin, said that they have cut prior authorization turnaround times by 60 percent and increased annual revenues by $3 million in the first year of using the system.

6.3.4   Claims status checks

Particularly in the U.S.A., providers often check the status of claims and prioritize high-value claims for payment. These checks add literally billions to administrative costs every year. According to an estimate by the Coalition for Affordable Quality Healthcare, in 2018 there were about 737 million claim status checks made by phone, web portal access, or fax— all time-consuming (14 minutes) and expensive (an estimated $7.12) methods for humans to employ. Many of them didn't result in actionable information and had to be repeated later (CAQH 2018).

Claims status checks are very well suited for RPA, which can check web portals or make calls as if it were a human user. Once it receives a claim status, it can automatically update a provider's financial systems. RPA systems are particularly good at reaching into multiple information systems and accessing and inputting information. Sarah Knodel, the revenue cycle head at BSWHealth, is using Waystar's RPA capabilities for status checks, with considerable savings in labor and expense. And as the

RPA system gets the claim status from payers, it automatically removes approved claims from the workflow of the hospital's claims collectors, allowing them to concentrate on the claims that need human attention.

6.3.5   Fraud, waste, and abuse

Most fraud (or "fraud, waste, and abuse" as it is often called) in healthcare payments is perpetrated against payers—either insurance companies or governments—and committed primarily by unscrupulous physicians. Preventing it is a priority for payers. The outcomes can be substantial; one large U.S. payer that chose not to be identified told us that they had used AI to reduce fraudulent payments by over a billion dollars per year. Highmark, a smaller insurer based in Pennsylvania, said that it has used AI and other tools to save $850 million over five years. The U.S. Centers for Medicare and Medicaid Services also has announced that it is using AI to detect fraudulent claims (Brady 2019).

Fraud reduction in the past was done by an army of clinician reviewers on a small sample of claims. AI can analyze a much larger number of claims, using some combination of ML, predictive analytics, rule engines, network analysis, outlier analysis, and unsupervised learning to identify anomalies. AI can be trained on data from past documented fraud claims, coding frequencies, and common attributes of fraudsters—both patients and physicians. Companies like Cotiviti, Codoxo, and Brighterion, a unit of Mastercard, supply payers with AI-based services and systems to detect fraud.

Though these applications of AI and automation may not be particularly exciting, they are among the most financially rewarding (not to mention the amount of tedium they eliminate). If countries like the U.S.A. are going to create and maintain such bureaucratic and fragmented payment systems, the participants might as well use these technologies to ease the burden.

6.4   External administrative relationships and AI

Many administrative challenges in healthcare arise when different organizations attempt to communicate and transact with one another. Providers communicate with insurance company payers and governments, physicians communicate with hospitals, hospitals communicate with labs, and so forth.

As the industry moves to adopt AI-based tools for these communications, we will encounter comical situations. Waystar, a vendor we mentioned earlier, has a system—a "bot"—that automatically makes calls to payers to learn the status of claims. Often, according to Matt Hawkins, the CEO of Waystar, the bot calling on behalf of the provider ends up talking to a bot at the payer. Having "your bot call my bot" is more efficient than humans calling humans, but of course it would be better if the respective systems of payers and providers could communicate with each other through direct interfaces.

This situation is all too common in administrative healthcare AI. AI is making administrative processes more efficient, but not nearly as efficient as they could be. Faxes are one key example. Jonathan Bush, formerly the CEO of electronic health record (EHR) company Athena Health, wrote an article in 2018 about using AI to deal with this perennial bane of the U.S. healthcare system. Physicians who did business with his company received more than 120 million faxes each year (and we doubt things have gotten much better since).

If faxes have important information in them, some human usually needs to enter it into a computer system. Athena figured out a way to use AI to extract the key information from a faxed document, categorize it, and automatically enter it into the right system. Athena saved medical practices an average of more than a minute per fax (from 2:36 to 1:11) and eliminated over three million hours of work from the healthcare system (Bush 2018).

This is great, of course, and far be it from us to criticize an AI application that saves so much money and time. But the healthcare industry *should not be using faxes*. To get value from a new technology, you often have to modernize other technology. Using AI to extract the critical data from faxes—or adopting other approaches to make a highly inefficient process more efficient on the margins—is a good short-term approach, but not one that will lead to prosperity over the long term.

6.5   Operational decision-making with AI

Name a task or process and there is probably an opportunity to make better decisions with machine learning, or to automate structured activities with RPA. Many of them involve optimizing the use of scarce resources. In healthcare, those include expensive rooms of various types, expensive machines of various types, and expensive (or even inexpensive) inventory of various types.

6.5.1   Operating rooms

Operating rooms (ORs) are scarce and valuable resources for many providers; one Stanford study suggested that they cost $62 per minute. Surgeons are even more expensive. AI is increasingly being used to schedule surgeries across OR and surgeon availability. The Mayo Clinic was a pioneer in this regard: as early as 2012 it began an effort to study and improve surgery scheduling (Ozen 2015). Its initial investigations found high levels of inefficiency in scheduling rooms and surgeons, with considerable surgeon overtime.

Data scientists at the Clinic gathered data from previous surgeries at the hospital, the time they took to perform, and contextual data like patient profiles, the time in surgery for specific surgeons, and OR variations. They created a complex machine learning algorithm that attempted to optimize available times for surgeries while minimizing overtime. A human surgery scheduler could then use a color-coded system to schedule optimum times for a patient based on available rooms and surgeons.

The Clinic conducted a pilot of the new algorithm and process from mid-2012 to mid-2013. During that time, it increased utilization for spine surgeries by 19 percent and reduced overtime by 10 percent. Other studies at Brigham & Women's Hospital in Boston and elsewhere have demonstrated that machine learning models can do a better job of estimating the duration of surgical cases than physician experience or electronic medical record systems (Tuwatananurak 2019).

Providers no longer need to have highly trained data scientists on staff to develop machine learning models for surgical scheduling. Various vendors provide AI-enabled tools for this purpose. Some also incorporate

AI-based recommendations for the equipment needed in the OR for each procedure.

For example, the Norwegian company Globus.AI has AI-based scheduling software for use by provider organizations. One of their customers, a medical staffing company called Dedicare, used the software to schedule about 4,500 shifts per week. According to Globus, the system saves about 90 percent of the time it takes to fill each available slot, saving a scheduling manager between two and four hours every day. Increased scheduling precision allows hospitals to increase their staffing capacity between 30 percent and 40 percent. During the Covid-19 pandemic, Globus offered its software for free to Norway's public hospitals (Kahn 2020).

6.5.2   Inpatient rooms

For hospital care, payers in the U.S.A. draw a distinction between "treatment rooms" (standard inpatient rooms) and "observation rooms" (often used for patients who have been treated in the emergency department or undergone a surgical procedure). The decision on which type of room to use for a given patient has implications for the length and cost of a stay, the type of care received, and the hospital's overall capacity. The rules surrounding reimbursement for one type of room versus the other can be complex. Patients are sometimes not assigned to the correct type of room for the care they require and need to be transferred later. An AI algorithm could keep track of all those complexities and optimize the decision for each patient's situation. A study of such an algorithm showed enough of an improvement that the hospital could theoretically handle almost 600 extra patients per year (Pachamanova 2021).

6.5.3   Equipment utilization

Radiology equipment is both expensive and profitable for providers, but the potential profit depends on keeping the equipment busy. No-shows incur significant opportunity costs. Massachusetts General Hospital developed an algorithm that predicts whether a particular patient is likely to show up for an appointment (Glover 2017). Massachusetts General researchers also developed an automated language translation system that translates radiology instructions for non-English-speaking patients; it resulted in a statistically significant reduction in variability of radiology procedure times for those patients.

Healthcare provider institutions have a diverse set of facilities and treat a diverse set of patients. We're confident that decisions using data and AI will ultimately lead to more efficient use of those facilities, and therefore to better and less expensive care, than decisions based on human experience and intuition.

6.6   AI in procurement and supply chain management

Hospital supplies are expensive. We're not just talking bandages and tongue depressors. A drug-eluting stent to treat coronary artery blockage costs a hospital several thousand dollars; a pacemaker can cost tens of thousands (typically much less in Europe, but still thousands). Drugs can cost over $10,000 per patient for a month's supply (again, often less in Europe). The consulting firm Guidehouse estimates that U.S. hospitals spend over $25 billion per year in unnecessary supply chain costs (Guidehouse 2019). All providers, regardless of nationality, need to stock appropriate supplies for patients' needs while minimizing excess inventory. The nature and complexity of the task is well suited to AI.

AI can improve healthcare supply chains in various ways, including:

- *Matching patient demand and supply.* Given enough data from the past, machine learning is usually the best way to predict how many patients, of what type and with what healthcare needs, will arrive at the hospital or doctor's office. Those predictions can be matched against supply inventories. The predictions won't be perfect, so supply chains will need to include some supplies beyond the predicted amount. But they are likely to be better than predictions achieved through other means.
- *Logistical planning for distributed care.* Care is moving from acute-care hospitals to a variety of other settings, from rehab facilities to clinics to patients' homes. AI can help supply chain managers optimize the transportation methods, frequency, and routing of supplies from manufacturers to warehouses to healthcare facilities to the end customer.
- *Ordering.* It's time-consuming (and mistake-prone) for humans to perform the administrative tasks in ordering and reordering supplies. AI—both robotic process automation and ML, or as their combi-

nation is sometimes known, "intelligent process automation"—can automatically check availability for backordered products, look up clinical equivalent drugs or devices, send out purchase orders and invoices, and match deliveries to invoices. AI is also increasingly being used to extract key terms from contracts and embed them in supply chain transaction systems as well as auditing processes. One AI startup, Kalderos, keeps track of all relevant drug discounts and assesses whether discounts are compliant with federal and local regulations in the U.S.A. (Landi 2020).

*   *Estimating likely supply use and costs for procedures.* Just as providers are using AI to estimate out-of-pocket costs for patients, they can also estimate likely costs for actual procedures in hospitals—called "cost-per-case capture." It's not uncommon for OR staff to forget to scan some supplies used during a procedure, or for a physician to change a procedure once it's underway. Machine learning models can alert staff that supplies expected to be used in a procedure were not on the report of supplies consumed. And just as AI can supply rapid estimates for patients, it can also provide estimates for physicians of the cost implications of a mid-course procedure change.

*   *Labor scheduling and optimization.* While labor costs for physicians, nurses, and technicians are not generally considered part of supply chain management, they have a large impact on provider and patient costs, and scheduling them is an exercise in matching supply and demand—the type of task at which AI excels. One company, Lightning Bolt Solutions, says it helps schedule over three million shift hours each month for 20,000 clinicians at over 400 healthcare organizations.

6.7   Case study: a provider with a broad administrative AI effort

Administrative and financial tasks are a primary focus of AI efforts at New York-Presbyterian Hospital (NYP), a New York City academic medical center whose quality of care is ranked among the best in the U.S.A. David Tsay, M.D., who was when interviewed the hospital's Associate Chief Transformation Officer (now at Apple Health), said that AI-enabled clinical processes will come soon enough, but he believed the "lowest hanging fruit" for AI are routine operations that support care delivery, especially manual, paper-based processes that may have been in place for decades.

Take, for example, radiology. Many startups and research labs have focused on AI-based image scanning and interpretation, which we discuss elsewhere. But Tsay noted that it typically takes a couple of weeks to get an appointment, secure authorization from an insurer, and make sure that the correct clinical data are available—all before a patient can get an x-ray. Improving those tasks would be of immediate benefit for the hospital's patients.

Tsay and his colleagues have partnered with RPA vendor WorkFusion (in which NYP has also invested) to improve administrative and financial processes by automating their workflows, as well as by improving decisions within those processes using ML algorithms. They have used this method to make the revenue cycle more efficient, ensure correct coding of diagnoses and treatments, and to reduce denials of insurance claims. Eventually, the hospital hopes to provide AI-based solutions for improving patient access and overall experience, including a chatbot for patient interface and an automated appointment-setting service.

RPA technology is well suited to the hospital's situation for a number of reasons. It has a lot of legacy systems, multiple electronic medical record systems and substantial "technical debt" (that is, difficulty implementing changes because of past programming decisions that favored ease of execution over technological rigor). Interfacing RPA to these systems allows for a more seamless patient experience without having to reprogram the systems themselves. The combination of RPA with natural language processing (NLP) capabilities enables the capture of key data in charts and clinical notes. The hospital has plenty of data in an enterprise warehouse and a data lake that can be used to train ML models. The data covers all aspects of care, including lab values, clinical procedures, diagnoses, and patient charges and bills.

NYP has also applied RPA and ML to clinical coding. The correct codes are important not only for billing and insurance claims, but also for understanding the care that a patient has received. The hospital has created a set of digital robots to scan through charts, look at diagnoses, and analyze related data. The robots both reduce the need for manual labor and improve coding accuracy by 20–30 percent. The hospital also uses the bots to review the work of human coders, which has further improved accuracy.

NYP uses RPA and ML capabilities to automate the processing of supplier invoices. The hospital receives hundreds of thousands of invoices a year in a variety of different formats. The RPA/ML system extracts key data from the invoices, compares it with data about the items the hospital actually received, flags any discrepancies, and forwards invoices for payment that have no discrepancies. The system learns from every new invoice format that it analyzes. Almost half of the invoices received are automatically processed, with higher percentages to come.

The hospital uses RPA to automate timekeeping for employees who forget to clock in: a process that used to take the employee 10 to 15 minutes and now takes virtually no time. Tsay said the system saved some costs on back-end reconciliation, but most importantly, it returned over 300,000 hours to frontline staff. That time is much better spent at the patient's bedside on clinical care.

Tsay noted that elimination of jobs has never been the hospital's focus. Instead, he said, the goal is to employ the technologies to help frontline staff work more effectively and productively. He commented:

> These systems let our frontline workers perform less mundane, repetitive tasks. Instead, they can work on an exception basis and deal with more complex issues. The work is less about finding that information needle in the haystack. Now it's found for you and the question becomes how to solve the core issue. It's a shift to higher-order work, and in many cases, it has required a fair amount of retraining. We're changing both the work itself and the change management process.

Though some employees were initially suspicious of these initiatives, they have increased job satisfaction, productivity, and the capacity to handle an ever-expanding workload. Tsay said developing the applications in the context of a broader transformation initiative, aligned with the core mission of the hospital, helps with change management and employee buy-in.

Any time demand needs to be matched to supply, any time documents need to be matched, any time key information needs to be extracted from documents, and any time structured, information-based tasks need to be performed, AI can come to the rescue. We can eliminate a vast amount of inefficiency and excess cost in healthcare systems around the world, and redirect the knowledge and experience of every healthcare worker away from administrative tedium and toward helping patients. Because of care innovations, aging populations, and broader access to medical information, the complexity of and demand for care increases every year. Only with AI technologies like those described in this chapter can we hope to satisfy that need.

References

AMA (2021). 2020 AMA Prior Authorization Survey. April. https://www.ama-assn.org/system/files/prior-authorization-survey.pdf.

Brady, M. (2019). CMS thinks artificial intelligence could help cut medicare fraud. *Modern Healthcare*, October 22. https://www.modernhealthcare.com/information-technology/cms-thinks-artificial-intelligence-could-help-cut-medicare-fraud.

Bush, J. (2018). How AI is taking the scut work out of health care. *Harvard Business Review*, March 5. https://hbr.org/2018/03/how-ai-is-taking-the-scut-work-out-of-health-care.

CAQH (2018). CAQH INDEX: a report of healthcare industry adoption of electronic business transactions and cost savings. https://www.caqh.org/sites/default/files/explorations/index/report/2018-index-report.pdf.

Cutler, D. (2020). Reducing administrative costs in U.S. health care. *The Hamilton Project/Brookings*, March. https://www.brookings.edu/wp-content/uploads/2020/03/Cutler_PP_LO.pdf.

Ellerbeck, A. (2021). The Health 202: hospitals drag feet on new regulations to disclose costs of medical services. *Washington Post*, January 25. https://www.washingtonpost.com/politics/2021/01/25/health-202-hospitals-drag-feet-new-regulations-disclose-costs-medical-services/.

Glover, M. IV, Daye, D., Khalilzadeh, O., et al. (2017). Socioeconomic and demographic predictors of missed opportunities to provide advanced imaging services. *Journal of the American College of Radiology*, 14(11): 1403–11. http://doi.org/10.1016/j.jacr.2017.05.015.

Guidehouse (2019). Annual hospital supply chain savings opportunity reaches $25.7 billion. November. https://guidehouse.com/-/media/www/site/insights/healthcare/2019/supply-chain-analysis-infographic.pdf.

Himmelstein, D.U., Campbell, T. and Woolhandler, S. (2020). Health care administrative costs in the United States and Canada, 2017. *Annals of Internal Medicine*, 172(2): 134–42. http://doi.org/10.7326/M19-2818 [published correction appears in *Annals of Internal Medicine*, 173(5): 415].

Kahn, J. (2020). 'Boring A.I.' may be the real lifesaver in this pandemic. *Fortune. com*, April 7. https://fortune.com/2020/04/07/how-a-i-will-be-a-lifesaver-in-coronavirus-pandemic/.

Landi, H. (2020). This health tech startup is trying to disrupt the drug discount system: here's how. *Fierce Healthcare,* December 16. https://www.fiercehealthcare.com/payer/health-tech-startup-trying-to-disrupt-drug-discount-system-here-s-how.

LaPointe, J. (2020). How artificial intelligence is optimizing revenue cycle management. *RevCycle Intelligence,* April 10. https://revcycleintelligence.com/features/how-artificial-intelligence-is-optimizing-revenue-cycle-management.

Ozen, A., Marmor, Y., Rohleder, T., et al. (2015). Optimization and simulation of orthopedic spine surgery cases at Mayo Clinic. *Manufacturing & Service Operations Management,* 18(1): 157–75. http://dx.doi.org/10.1287/msom.2015.0564.

Pachamanova, D., Tilson, V. and Dwyer-Matzky, K. (2021). A data-driven approach to improving hospital observation unit operations. *INFORMS Transactions on Education,* May 27. https://doi.org/10.1287/ited.2021.0251cs.

Tuwatananurak, J.P., Zadeh, S., Xu, X., et al. (2019). Machine learning can improve estimation of surgical case duration: a pilot study. *Journal of Medical Systems,* 43(3): 44. http://doi.org/10.1007/s10916-019-1160-5.

7 The impacts of AI on human healthcare providers

7.1   Introduction

No issue surrounding AI is more important than its impact on people. In addition to patients, doctors, nurses, technicians, pharmacists, administrators, orderlies—even senior executives—will all be impacted in various ways. In its 2019 report "AI and the Health Care Workforce," the American Hospital Association said:

> Artificial intelligence and its first and second cousins, machine learning and robotic process automation, respectively, will fundamentally change how most everyone working in hospitals and health systems will do their jobs in the future. (AHA 2019)

This issue attracts plenty of media hype. This chapter will look beyond the hype and clarify how people in healthcare are already being affected, what's likely to happen as adoption increases, and also what's highly unlikely to happen. Preparing for these changes can't take place overnight, and provider executives must anticipate and plan.

7.2   Healthcare job loss from AI

Let's get one controversial issue out of the way quickly: though it's impossible to prove with statistics, it seems unlikely that a single doctor or nurse has lost a job because of AI. And it's not because AI hasn't been around for a while; clinical decision support systems, the rules-based first generation of healthcare AI, were introduced in the 1970s. AI has automated tasks and improved productivity (or at least, that has been the intention), but it doesn't seem to have put any clinicians out of work, and we posit that it won't, or at least not anytime soon. Why?

First, AI performs individual tasks and does not yet address all the tasks that every clinician performs. Many have predicted, for example, that AI-enabled image-reading will put radiologists out of work, but that's only one of the ten or more tasks in the radiologist's job description (Langlotz 2019). And so far, AI image-reading is itself limited: any given algorithm can read and interpret some images, but typically only for a narrow set of diseases or healthcare problems (Davenport 2018).

Second, AI isn't yet incorporated into clinical workflows. In radiology, where use of AI is relatively advanced (as we have discussed elsewhere), there aren't enough AI use cases yet to enable a broad set of AI-driven clinical activities by practicing radiologists. That's even more true in other specialties such as pathology. A variety of research findings suggest that deep learning image recognition can be very effective across different fields of cell pathology, but there are as yet no such systems in clinical practice, in part because of a lack of data standards, which are well established in radiology but do not exist for pathology (Acs 2020).

Third, it's too early to understand how jobs will be eliminated, changed, or created. What Stanford economist Erik Brynjolfsson calls "digital capital"—change in business processes, skills, job definitions, and the like—has yet to be developed to support AI in healthcare or for that matter in most other industries (Brynjolfsson 2021). Many of these types of changes were implemented for the rules-based clinical decision support generation of AI (Boxwala 2011) but have not yet been created for more algorithmic and data-intensive forms of AI. In that previous generation, new jobs such as "knowledge engineer" were created to extract knowledge from clinicians; we can expect similar new roles for the newer forms of AI.

These three arguments seem to suggest that AI isn't quite ready to replace human beings in the healthcare setting. But after a few more years of technical and digital capital development, will doctors and nurses start losing their jobs? We think not, for several reasons.

First, as we'll discuss below, there aren't nearly enough clinicians to begin with. Second, clinicians, payers, and regulators seem to prefer thinking about AI as a "second set of eyes" rather than as the only clinical observer or decision maker. They're fine with AI systems doing a first pass or a confirmatory one on a diagnosis or a radiology image interpretation, but they are reluctant to turn the entire process over to a machine, which brings up issues of transparency, accountability, and liability that they are not yet ready to address.

Finally, patients may continue to prefer human providers. A small survey in the U.K. found that most patients preferred having a human doctor, though they were comfortable with that doctor consulting an AI system (British Heart Foundation 2018). A larger survey in Europe found some-what negative attitudes toward AI replacing human healthcare providers (Chen 2020). Even in China, where AI in healthcare is better established than most other countries, less than half of posts in a social media analysis expected that AI would either fully or partially replace human doctors at some point (Gao 2020).

7.3   There's a healthcare labor shortage coming anyway

There is already a worldwide shortage of healthcare providers, and it is expected to get worse. In the U.S.A., the Association of American Medical Colleges expects an estimated shortage of between 37,800 and 124,000 physicians by 2034, including shortfalls in both primary and specialty care (AAMC 2021). In the U.K., the British Medical Association expects a shortage of almost 50,000 doctors over the next 20 years (BMA 2021). Europe already has a shortage of doctors, particularly in rural areas (Berthier 2018). Globally, the World Health Organization (WHO) pre-dicts a shortage of nine million clinicians by 2030, even with 40 million new clinician jobs added (WHO 2016).

Thus far there is little evidence of any country using AI to mitigate the impact of these shortages. While AI could augment the available clinical personnel, such an effort would require establishing new clinical work-flows and new regulatory and payment structures, and training doctors and nurses now on how best to use AI in their practices.

7.4   Which jobs can be automated?

Even if jobs will not be replaced in large numbers by AI, there will surely be differences among healthcare professions in terms of the ease and scope of work automation. There have already been efforts to categorize work tasks in terms of how likely they are to be automatable. The well-known Oxford Martin Institute classification in 2013, for example, predicted that 47 percent of U.S. jobs are subject to automation (Frey 2013). A generalization of this classification approach is found in the "suitability for machine learning" analysis from the MIT Initiative on the Digital Economy (Brynjolfsson 2018). This approach is laudable in that it does break jobs down into constituent tasks, but predictions using it thus far have not generally been accurate.

This type of prediction has been extended to specific healthcare jobs. A McKinsey study, for example, classified jobs in an analysis of the impact of AI on healthcare jobs in Europe (McKinsey 2020). Instead of the percentage of automatable tasks, it focused on the percentage of work hours of each job type that could be automated. It found that "family and general practitioners" have the highest percentage of automatable hours among physicians. However, that number was still low—only 12 percent. Those tasks presumably included taking basic vital signs, which can increasingly be done by patients themselves. However, it seems quite possible that general practitioners will eventually add a role—integrators and interpreters of AI-based knowledge—that would increase their importance rather than diminishing it. Algorithms will provide information on various aspects of a disease or condition, but the patient will rely on the physician to make sense of it all.

Physical positioning of patients is an example of an "unpredictable physical" task—a factor that diminishes the likelihood of automation in the McKinsey study. Chiropractors have the lowest percentage of automatable work hours—2 percent—among all clinicians. Patient positioning to ensure clear airways—another unpredictable physical task—is also a responsibility of anesthesiologists, who were rated at 10 percent of automatable hours. This may explain in part why an automated anesthesiology machine called Sedasys was approved by the U.S. Food and Drug Administration (FDA) in 2013 and introduced to the market, but withdrawn in 2016 because of a low level of adoption (Goudra 2017). Empathy and understanding of mental health ("interfacing with stakeholder" tasks) also seem to be in short supply among machines; psychiatrists had the fewest automatable hours among physicians.

Specialists such as radiologists and pathologists who do not normally see patients in person may be more affected by AI. Image interpretation is a substantial component of their jobs, and they often communicate with patients and other physicians through reports that could be automatically generated. As we have pointed out, however, these specialists do perform a number of tasks that are not likely to be automated soon.

Clinical professionals whose primary focus is caring for patients across a broad spectrum of needs, such as nurses, seem unlikely to be greatly affected by AI. Those who primarily provide diagnosis and advice, such as physicians, seem more likely to be affected. It may be that AI moves some physicians more in the direction of patient care rather than gathering, interpreting, and reporting on information. And if regulations allow it, diagnosis and prescription may increasingly be taken over by nurses working with AI systems.

If any jobs are to be lost because of AI and related automation capabilities, they are probably most likely to involve administrative workers in healthcare rather than clinical ones. As we have discussed in Chapter 6, administrative applications are the "low hanging fruit" for AI in healthcare. They are more likely to involve technologies like robotic process automation than sophisticated deep learning models. As such, they are relatively easy to develop and don't require regulatory approval to implement. Although we don't see much evidence of job loss yet in coding, billing, appointment scheduling, and other such administrative domains, we do expect it at some point. As we have discussed, such job losses would not be good for the individuals involved, but they do hold the potential of reducing the cost of healthcare, particularly in administratively complex countries like the U.S.A.

7.5   Working alongside AI

We expect that most healthcare jobs will not be replaced by AI, but augmented by it. Given what is happening in jobs in other domains and to some degree already in healthcare, we can predict what certain jobs will be like when clinicians have AI as a colleague.

7.5.1 Less reaction, more prediction

AI, particularly in the form of machine learning (ML), is a predictive technology. Healthcare has largely been a reactive discipline. Someone gets sick, a clinician reacts with an intervention of some type, and the patient recovers—or not. But AI-based healthcare, if done well, predicts health problems in patients before they occur, or at least before it is too late to do anything about it. For example, researchers at the University of Pittsburgh Medical Center are predicting a variety of musculoskeletal diseases (osteoarthritis, knee replacement, etc.) based primarily on radiology images, and are working with patients to treat some problems with drugs and others with early surgical interventions (Kundu 2020). One AI software company, KenSci, based in Seattle, Washington, says it can predict the likelihood of disease hotspots and heavy care utilizers, disease progression, inpatient deterioration, sepsis, length of stay, readmission, and end of life—as well as their implications for staffing, emergency department availability, and no-shows—all with ML tools and a "prediction platform."

To make use of this predictive technology, providers would have to be prepared with treatment protocols for the predicted medical problems (ideally built into the electronic health record (EHR) system and tied to the predictions), and they would have to be able to explain to patients how the AI "knows" what's going to happen to them. Providers would need to understand the assumptions behind the models and to know how they were trained. They would have to become more accustomed to explaining probabilistic models to patients, so that patients could make informed decisions about whether to proceed with medical interventions.

7.5.2 Less deciding, more checking

A common pattern with AI in other fields is that it takes over many primary decision-making tasks, and humans check the decisions to make sure they're reasonable. In this role, any user needs to be trained to recognize and deal with an unreasonable decision. Applying AI in this way in healthcare could offload many routine decisions, but doing it safely will require meticulous decision-checking.

If AI becomes better than the average physician at aspects of diagnosis and treatment, it may make sense to put the primary decision load on the machine, with physicians (or possibly nurses or physician assistants) playing the checking role. This role may be difficult for some doctors to accept. Clinical decision support systems, the earliest version of this type of AI, elicited many complaints of "cookbook medicine," and more sophisticated applications may spark even more complaints. While this application of AI holds a lot of potential, it represents a big cultural change that organizations should approach with caution.

7.5.3   Less waste, more efficiency

A lot of healthcare services are wasted. Patients see doctors, or even visit hospital emergency rooms, when they don't need to. Drugs—particularly antibiotics—are prescribed and consumed when they shouldn't be. Some forms of waste in healthcare—poor care coordination, for example—may not be addressed directly by AI, but the waste category of "overtreatment or low-value care" could easily be improved with the technology. By one estimate, waste in healthcare delivery costs the U.S.A. between $75.7 billion and $101.2 billion per year (Shrank 2019). We discussed administrative waste in the previous chapter, but the direct waste of care is significant as well.

How could AI help reduce waste? In Chapter 4 we described Ping An's Good Doctor application, the most widely used medical smartphone app in the world, which "discusses" symptoms with patients to determine whether a doctor visit is necessary. Doctors can prescribe medications over the app without an office visit.

These systems—sometimes referred to as "Internet hospitals"—are beginning to be studied by researchers. One recent analysis concluded that they can improve efficiency:

> … [I]nternet hospitals played the role of the family doctor, which helped to relieve the stress placed on offline hospitals and facilitated people's lives. In addition, good user experiences, especially regarding disease-related inquisitions, suggested that online health services can help solve health problems. (Jiang 2021)

Although the AI-assisted care model is already pervasive in China, it has yet to be employed widely in other parts of the world. We expect that its usage will grow, that there will be multiple approaches and AI technologies investigated, and that it will ultimately lead to less waste and more efficiency.

7.5.4   Less administration, more care

As we discussed in the previous chapter, healthcare is riddled with wasteful "administrative complexity." We've already described ways that AI can save money and time by taking over and often streamlining administration, but we've only touched on what a welcome change this would be for healthcare providers, who spend way too much of their time performing administrative tasks.

7.5.5   Less routine care, more complex care

In other industries, AI "picks off" common, routine tasks, leaving the more complex ones for human beings. This will be a likely pattern in healthcare as well. Physician offices and clinics see many routine problems: colds and other upper respiratory infections and viruses, ear infections, joint pain, back pain. Diagnosis and treatment of these simple ailments could easily be done with AI, even in its current state, leaving human clinicians to handle more complex cases requiring an office or hospital visit. This change would allow them to practice more regularly at the top of their license: a perennial goal for increasing clinician job satisfaction (Schirle 2019; Friedberg 2013).

7.5.6   Less facility care, more home care

AI will also ease the process of monitoring and treating patients at home (or at work or in a car or walking down the street). Remote patient monitoring and wearable sensors, as we've mentioned elsewhere, will make it much easier to gather and analyze patient data. AI systems can monitor the data and alert patients and clinicians if a face-to-face visit (in a medical office, hospital, or the home) is necessary. Provider executives may want to temper their plans for expansion of physical facilities for patients; they may not be as necessary in the future.

7.5.7   Less human touch, more robot touch

As we have discussed elsewhere, we are already seeing the rise of surgical robots for common surgeries such as knee and hip replacements, prostate surgery, and gall bladder removal. Robotic surgery is increasing at a rapid rate, accounting for 15 percent of all surgical procedures in one U.S. study (Sheetz 2020). It seems likely that this trend will continue and be applied to other types of surgery. And while human surgeons are still "driving" the surgical robot, greater degrees of autonomy are likely to be on the way (Attanasio 2021). Robots are also likely to take on some nursing functions, such as ambulation support, measurement of vital signs, medication administration, and adherence to infectious disease protocols (Robert 2019). They are also changing the role of pharmacists and pharmacy technicians in provider organizations, taking over many packaging and distribution activities (Davenport 2021).

7.5.8   Less guessing, more evidence

Numerous studies suggest that many healthcare decisions are not evidence-based. In one study of U.S. hospitals, more than half of Chief Nursing Officers reported that evidence-based medicine is practiced in their organization either "not at all" or only "somewhat" (Melnyk 2016). Clinicians guess, or rely on dimly remembered maxims from medical school. The trend toward evidence-based medicine began several decades ago with clinical decision support systems and quality measurement programs. But analytics and AI can bring substantially more evidence and knowledge to healthcare decision-making. Not only do evidence and knowledge inform AI algorithms and rules, but automation can help ensure that data-driven decisions are made. Many early clinical decision support systems focused on averting drug interactions and flagging common misdiagnoses. ML could make those recommendations more personalized and better rooted in current data.

7.6   New skills

These new processes and roles will, of course, require new skills. Healthcare will have to follow other industries that are upskilling and reskilling their employees for AI. It's still early days for this type of training, but courses are beginning to be offered, particularly in a few AI-oriented specialty areas. For example, the Radiological Society of North America has announced an imaging AI certificate that radiologists can earn online.

However, such programs are still relatively rare. They are largely absent in other fields where AI is increasingly capable of image analysis, such as pathology (Arora 2021) and ophthalmology (Valikodath 2021). Professional associations in these specialties need to move quickly to improve specialists' awareness and skills.

If decisions or recommendations are to be made by AI algorithms, clinicians will need to understand—at least at a high level—how they were arrived at and whether they can be trusted. In image-oriented systems, it will be particularly challenging to interpret results and to explain them to patients. Since different specialties have different typical use cases and algorithms for addressing them, each specialty will need its own training programs. Some will have more difficulty than others. For example, the deep learning neural networks typically used to do image analysis are difficult to understand even for data scientists. In more traditional ML algorithms used for prediction, it is normally possible to determine what variables or features are most influential in the model, and even how important they are in a prediction for a specific case.

More generally, digital skills are at the core of being able to make effective use of AI. Many physicians and nurses found it difficult to transition to electronic medical record systems, and still use antiquated communications technologies like fax machines. Although many medical schools offer courses in "clinical informatics" or similar topics, they are rarely part of the required curriculum for physicians-in-training. A few schools have adapted their curricula to a highly digital environment—one German school, for example, has a "Medicine in the Digital Age" curriculum (Kuhn 2020)—but these are still rare. In 2016 a European Union committee proposed mandatory programs in digital skills for health professionals, but the recommendation was not adopted (Dalati 2016). Perhaps the dramatic rise in telehealth technologies during the Covid pandemic will bring about faster and broader adoption of digital health education that can include AI.

There will also need to be hiring and training for the AI skills involved in creating, configuring, and maintaining AI models. Organizations will need more data scientists and data engineers, as well as more "translator" roles (to mediate between different healthcare settings and AI developers and vendors). As these types of positions are often difficult to fill, it will be wise for most large organizations to develop such skills among existing employees in addition to hiring them from the outside.

7.7   Messages to employees

While we believe that the impacts of AI on healthcare employment will be relatively minor during the 2020s, that doesn't mean that employees won't worry about keeping their jobs. Employers should make clear their positions on AI—ideally telling employees that job loss from AI is not expected in the near term. If there are areas of the organization where AI may in fact lead to significant job losses—routine administrative roles, for example—affected employees should be informed as soon as possible of the timeframe and options. Given the value of an employee who knows the organization and the potential difficulty of filling other roles, those options should include retraining whenever possible.

We also feel that employees should be informed that AI is coming, and that it will lead to considerable changes in many of their jobs. Because the impact of AI will vary widely across the organization, different specialty areas and administrative departments should be encouraged to have discussions and study groups about how AI might affect that particular domain and what employees should be doing to prepare. Employees should also be presented with options for how to learn about AI and its impact. Senior executives in provider and payer institutions should receive education on AI and how it will transform healthcare. The most effective organizations outside of healthcare in reskilling employees are those who provide resources, guidelines, and skill pathways, without forcing employees into directions in which they are not interested or comfortable.

It's natural for employees to feel both excitement and concern about AI. It is incumbent on organizations and their leaders to ease their concerns and channel their excitement into productive and beneficial outcomes.

References

AAMC (2021). AAMC report reinforces mounting physician shortage. Press release, June 11. https://www.aamc.org/news-insights/press-releases/aamc -report-reinforces-mounting-physician-shortage.

Acs, B., Rantalainen, M. and Hartman, J. (2020). Artificial intelligence as the next step towards precision pathology. *Journal of Internal Medicine*, 288(1): 62–81. http://doi.org/10.1111/joim.13030.

AHA (2019). AI and the health care workforce. September. https://www.aha.org/system/files/media/file/2019/09/Market_Insights_AI_Workforce_2.pdf.

Arora, A. and Arora, A. (2021). Pathology training in the age of artificial intelligence. *Journal of Clinical Pathology*, 74(2): 73–5. http://doi.org/10.1136/jclinpath-2020-207110.

Attanasio, A., et al. (2021). Autonomy in surgical robotics. *Annual Review of Control, Robotics, and Autonomous Systems*, May. https://www.annualreviews.org/doi/10.1146/annurev-control-062420-090543.

BMA (2021). Medical staffing in England: a defining moment for doctors and patients. July. https://www.bma.org.uk/media/4316/bma-medical-staffing -report-in-england-july-2021.pdf.

Boxwala, A.A., Rocha, B.H., Maviglia, S., et al. (2011). A multi-layered framework for disseminating knowledge for computer-based decision support. *Journal of the American Medical Informatics Association*, 18 (Suppl. 1): i132–i139. https://www.ncbi.nlm.nih.gov/pmc/articles/PMC3241169/.

British Heart Foundation (2018). Putting patients at the heart of artificial intelligence, report summary, https://www.bhf.org.uk/appg-summary-final.

Brynjolfsson, E. (2021). Digitization, data, and digital capital. Presentation delivered at the University of Waterloo, February 2. https://uwaterloo.ca/uwaterloo -centre-for-information-system-assurance/sites/ca.uwaterloo-centre-for -information-system-assurance/files/uploads/files/erik_brynjolfsson_- _digitization_data_and_digital_capital.pdf.

Brynjolfsson, E., Mitchell, T. and Rock, D. (2018). What can machines learn, and what does it mean for occupations and the economy? *MIT Initiative on the Digital Economy Research Brief*, Vol. 4. https://ide.mit.edu/wp-content/uploads/2018/12/2018-08-MITIDE-researchbrief-Erikb.final_.pdf.

Chen, Y.Y., Li, Y. and Li, C.J. (2020). Could artificial intelligence make human doctors obsolete? A survey based on public attitudes. *Eurpean Journal of Public Health*, 30(Suppl. 5). https://doi.org/10.1093/eurpub/ckaa166.040.

Dalati, F. et al. (2016). Digital skills for health professionals. *European Health Parliament*. https://www.healthparliament.eu/wp-content/uploads/2017/09/Digital-skills-for-health-professionals.pdf.

Davenport, T. (2021). The future of work now: pharmacists and the robotic pharmacy at Stanford Health Care. *Forbes.com*, January 18. https://www.forbes .com/sites/tomdavenport/2021/01/18/the-future-of-work-now-pharmacists -and-the-robotic-pharmacy-at-stanford-health-care/?sh=3f5164439376.

Davenport, T. and Dreyer, K. (2018). AI will change radiology but it won't replace radiologists. *Harvard Business Review*, March 27. https://hbr.org/2018/03/ai -will-change-radiology-but-it-wont-replace-radiologists.

Frey, C.-B. and Osborne, M. (2013). The future of employment: how susceptible are jobs to computerisation? *Oxford Martin Institute*, September 17. https://www.oxfordmartin.ox.ac.uk/downloads/academic/The_Future_of_Employment.pdf.

Friedberg, M. et al. (2013). Factors affecting physician professional satisfaction and their implications for patient care, health systems, and health policy. *RAND Health/AMA*. https://www.rand.org/content/dam/rand/pubs/research_reports/RR400/RR439/RAND_RR439.pdf.

Gao, S., He, L., Chen, Y., Li, D. and Lai, K. (2020). Public perception of artificial intelligence in medical care: content analysis of social media. *Journal of Medical Internet Research*, 22(7): e16649. http://doi.org/10.2196/16649.

Goudra, B. and Singh, P.M. (2017). Failure of Sedasys: destiny or poor design? *Anesthesia & Analgesia*, 124(2): 686–8. http://doi.org/10.1213/ANE.0000000000001643.

Jiang, X., Xie, H., Tang, R., et al. (2021). Characteristics of online health care services from China's largest online medical platform: cross-sectional survey study. *Journal of Medical Internet Research*, 23(4): e25817. https://pubmed.ncbi.nlm.nih.gov/33729985/.

Kuhn, S., Müller, N., Kirchgässner, E., Ulzheimer, L. and Deutsch, K.L. (2020). Digital skills for medical students – qualitative evaluation of the curriculum 4.0 'Medicine in the digital age.' *GMS Journal for Medical Education*, 37(6): Doc60. https://www.egms.de/static/en/journals/zma/2020-37/zma001353.shtml.

Kundu, S., et al. (2020). Enabling early detection of osteoarthritis from presymptomatic cartilage texture maps via transport-based learning. *PNAS*, 117(40): 24709–19. https://doi.org/10.1073/pnas.1917405117.

Langlotz, C.P. (2019). Will artificial intelligence replace radiologists? *Radiology: Artificial Intelligence*, 1(3): e190058. https://pubs.rsna.org/doi/full/10.1148/ryai.2019190058.

McKinsey (2020). Transforming healthcare with AI: the impact on the workforce and the organisation. https://www.mckinsey.com/~/media/McKinsey/Industries/Healthcare%20Systems%20and%20Services/Our%20Insights/Transforming%20healthcare%20with%20AI/Transforming-healthcare-with-AI.ashx.

Melnyk, B.M., Gallagher-Ford, L., Thomas, B.K., Troseth, M., Wyngarden, K. and Szalacha, L. (2016). A study of Chief Nurse Executives indicates low prioritization of evidence-based practice and shortcomings in hospital performance metrics across the United States. *Worldviews on Evidence-Based Nursing*, 13(1): 6–14. https://pubmed.ncbi.nlm.nih.gov/26873371/.

Robert, N. (2019). How artificial intelligence is changing nursing. *Nursing Management*, 50(9): 30–39. https://journals.lww.com/nursingmanagement/fulltext/2019/09000/how_artificial_intelligence_is_changing_nursing.8.aspx

Schirle, L., McCabe, B.E. and Mitrani, V. (2019). The relationship between practice environment and psychological ownership in advanced practice nurses. *Western Journal of Nursing Research*, 41(1): 6–24. https://pubmed.ncbi.nlm.nih.gov/29357756/.

Sheetz, K.H., Claflin, J. and Dimick, J.B. (2020). Trends in the adoption of robotic surgery for common surgical procedures. *JAMA Network Open*, 3(1): e1918911. https://jamanetwork.com/journals/jamanetworkopen/fullarticle/2758472.

Shrank, W.H., Rogstad, T.L. and Parekh, N. (2019). Waste in the US health care system: estimated costs and potential for savings. *JAMA Network*, 322(15): 1501–9. https://jamanetwork.com/journals/jama/article-abstract/2752664.

Valikodath, N.G., Cole, E., Ting, D.S.W., et al. (2021). Impact of artificial intelligence on medical education in ophthalmology. *Translational Vision, Science & Technology*, 10(7): 14. https://tvst.arvojournals.org/article.aspx?articleid=2772703.

WHO (2016). Global strategy on human resources for health: workforce 2030. https://www.who.int/hrh/resources/global_strategy_workforce2030_14_print.pdf.

8 Recognizing and managing AI-associated risks

8.1 Introduction

We have discussed a wide range of AI applications. The current and future users of these applications will find that, like most products and services, AI doesn't always fulfill its promises. Unlike some, its shortcomings may be subtle and escape notice until they cause major problems. They may stem from bugs, or they may happen when the AI is performing exactly as designed, because of design flaws rather than programming error. As with any new technology, AI poses risks that users must recognize and manage.

8.1.1 Overpromising/underdelivering

The presence of AI capabilities in a commercial product—even a very widely used one—is no guarantee that they have been exhaustively tested and will perform as the vendor claims. Epic Systems, one of the world's largest vendors of electronic health record systems, has at this writing built several AI-based capabilities into its products. But customers are finding that they're not working as expected, according to an investigation by STAT News.

For example, multiple Epic customers had complaints about its sepsis algorithm because it was delivering inaccurate and often irrelevant information. A team at the University of Michigan measured the algorithm in the real world with more than 27,000 patients at its medical center, representing almost 35,000 hospitalizations, and found that it missed cases at a much higher rate than Epic had promised based on pre-market testing, and sounded the sepsis alarm far too frequently for non-septic patients. "The widespread adoption of the [Epic Sepsis Model] despite its poor performance raises fundamental concerns about sepsis management on a national level," the team concluded in a study that appeared in *JAMA Internal Medicine* (Wong 2021).

One possible problem, according to the STAT investigation: One of the model's data points for a sepsis prediction—whether a physician had prescribed antibiotics for the patient—caught cases that human clinicians had already identified through other means. It was a successful prediction, but not a useful one (Ross 2021c).

8.1.2   Brittleness

Even when apparently intelligent, AI is often "brittle." A small change in what it thinks it "knows" can cause it to make mistakes: sometimes disastrous ones. An AI that learns to excel at a game against a human opponent may become confused and throw the game if the human starts actively trying to lose. A deep learning system—a technology that is particularly brittle—that can recognize a stop sign may misinterpret it as "Speed Limit 45" if some prankster has decorated it with a few stickers (Heaven 2019). AI often can't easily pivot away from what it was designed to do, even to take up a task that seems to a human to be almost the same.

One example of brittleness in healthcare AI was the spectacular failure of IBM's Watson initiative, which all but promised to cure cancer when it was introduced. Watson's first public triumph was a 2011 victory against a panel of champions on the U.S. trivia show *Jeopardy!* IBM marketing materials promised that Watson's abilities could be extended to sifting through genomic data of cancer patients to identify which of the thousands of available treatment combinations would be most effective, making it an indispensable oncologist's assistant.

It turned out that an AI purpose-built to win a quiz show could not be easily repurposed for making complex medical treatment decisions (Lohr 2021; Ross 2021a). After years of largely fruitless collaboration with major cancer centers, Watson has achieved some smaller successes: Watson Insights for Medical Literature does intelligent journal searches, and Watson for Genomics produces reports on patients' genomic data (Strickland 2019). These are modest wins compared with the initial aspirations. IBM agreed to sell Watson Health to Francisco Partners, a private equity firm, in January 2022.

8.2   Categories of risk

Both AI and medical knowledge are evolving quickly. When we combine these factors with the life-and-death decisions involved in the delivery of healthcare, we encounter unusual types and levels of risk not faced by (for example) an online store making product recommendations. Will clinicians trust an AI application to help them make decisions, or even make decisions for them? *Should* they trust it? Who is liable if AI causes medical error? Can AI-enabled applications compromise patients' privacy or data security?

We will discuss three general categories of AI risk that healthcare organizations must plan to manage. The first one, algorithm risk, is unique to AI-enabled products. The others—regulatory and liability—are not unique to AI-enabled products, but these products present some unique challenges, and the regulatory and legal environment will evolve as AI-enabled products come into common use.

8.3   Algorithm risk

Algorithm risk occurs when an algorithm does not correspond adequately with the reality that it's supposed to simulate or predict. No algorithm is a perfect parallel of reality, but it needs to be as close as possible for the aspects that matter. An application for screening breast images needs to distinguish among healthy tissue, precancerous lesions, and cancer. An algorithm that translates a CT scan into a 3D-printed model for planning a surgery has a more complex task: it must differentiate many kinds of tissues, including muscle, fat, bone, and skin, and distinguish all of these from the growth that the surgical team wants to remove. The more fully an algorithm must mirror reality in order to function, the greater the likelihood that it will fail to do so in some way.

Algorithm risk can have life-or-death implications for some medical applications, such as those that guide physicians' diagnostic or treatment decisions, or those that manage a device attached to a patient. Algorithm risk can also cause complications in operational or financial applications.

Algorithm risk never truly goes away, even after an apparently successful implementation, because like human intelligence, AI faces changing realities to which it may or may not be able to adapt. It is incumbent upon healthcare executives as well as their AI experts to continually monitor whether the world has changed in ways that are not reflected in their algorithms.

8.3.1 Covid prediction: how algorithms can go wrong

The Covid-19 pandemic offers a prime example of what can go wrong in developing algorithms to steer healthcare decisions. The need was urgent—there was no existing model for treatment and clinicians were trying increasingly desperate measures with no way to gauge their likelihood of success. And with thousands of newly hospitalized patients every day, the amount of available data should have been adequate to draw some conclusions and give clinicians direction, if only they had time to sift through it all. It was a situation tailor-made for the type of help that AI could provide, and hundreds of developers stepped up to the challenge.

However, several comprehensive reviews, encompassing hundreds of algorithms, failed to identify any that were actually useful, and some of them were downright misleading (Wynants 2020; Roberts 2021; Ross 2021d).

What went wrong?

> *Poor quality data.* Databases were hastily constructed, leading to mislabeled data and data from unknown sources. Datasets were combined from multiple sources, leading to duplication. In the U.S.A., Covid cases and deaths were measured differently across different states and even counties (Davenport 2020).
> *No separation of data.* Tools were trained and tested on the same data, violating the "external validation" requirement for algorithm testing,

and creating the impression that the algorithms were more accurate than they really were.

Irrelevant data. An algorithm interpreted printing on radiology images (the patient's name and medical record number, for example) as part of the image. It therefore used the font of the printing as a data point. A hospital with sicker patients happened to use a larger font, leading the algorithm to erroneously correlate large type with more severe illness.

Noncomparable data. Some image-reading algorithms were trained on datasets that included images where Covid-19 was suspected but not confirmed, which meant they couldn't reliably confirm when a patient had Covid. A few models intended to detect Covid pneumonia in adult chest x-rays were tested using images from children's x-rays. Hence the algorithm's training didn't teach it to recognize adult Covid pneumonia, though it learned to identify whether the patient was a child.

These types of problems are fixable. However, algorithm developers may lack the medical training to understand the data and thus its shortcomings. Conversely, the developer may have the appropriate medical training but lack the necessary AI algorithm knowledge. Your organization may not develop its own algorithms, but it may purchase AI-enabled products from vendors who face these types of data and process problems, fail to detect or fix them, and hide them from customers under the pretext of protecting their intellectual property.

Healthcare leaders should be aware of several other types of algorithm risk. Below we discuss three of them: bias, poor testing, and lack of transparency.

8.3.2 Bias

Algorithmic bias occurs when an algorithm produces results that are systematically skewed: for example, a facial recognition algorithm that struggles to accurately recognize the faces of non-white people because it was trained on white faces (Buolamwini 2018).

Biased algorithms can exacerbate real-life biases. A popular analytics program used in the U.S.A. to target patients for enhanced care management, to control chronic diseases and improve their health while reducing their overall cost of care, dramatically over-identified white patients compared with black ones who were less healthy by almost any measure. The bias arose because the measure that the algorithm relied on—total costs of the patient's care—missed race-related disparities in access to care, according to an independent analysis (Obermeyer 2019). Said the authors:

> At a given risk score, Black patients are considerably sicker than White patients, as evidenced by signs of uncontrolled illnesses. Remedying this disparity would increase the percentage of Black patients receiving additional help from 17.7 to 46.5%. The bias arises because the algorithm predicts health care costs rather than illness, but unequal access to care means that we spend less money caring for Black patients than for White patients. Thus, despite health care cost appearing to be an effective proxy for health by some measures of predictive accuracy, large racial biases arise (p. 447).

Bias in healthcare AI can occur for several reasons (Pratt 2020). Most of the time it has at least partly to do with data problems, including:

Skewed data. The data used to train a machine learning algorithm does not adequately reflect the algorithm's target population. Amazon, for example, had a hiring algorithm that favored applicants based on words like "executed" or "captured" that were more commonly found on men's resumes. The data used to develop the algorithm was dominated by men's resumes (Dastin 2018) and did not reflect the proportion of men's and women's resumes.

Old data. If the data used are not current, the world may have evolved in ways that make the sample data less and less a reflection of reality. For example, algorithms that attempted to predict the likelihood that a Covid patient would become very sick would need to be retrained on new data over the course of the pandemic to reflect advances in treatment, prevention (masks and vaccines) and virus variants.

Not enough data. If the training dataset is not large enough, there might be too few cases in the data to make meaningful conclusions about all the cases. This type of bias can happen when algorithms are applied to rare diseases.

Poorly understood data. The racial bias study at the beginning of this section offers a good example of this. A developer might assume that high healthcare costs or frequent utilization of health services are a good proxy for severity of illness. Using these criteria to flag the sickest patients will cause the algorithm to ignore potentially important groups: not only racial groups that face systemic lack of access to care, but people who don't have insurance and therefore don't seek routine care, or people who are so sick that they are receiving only palliative care. And it may erroneously flag patients who are relatively healthy but have temporarily high costs and utilization because they've had a joint replacement or are recovering from a sports injury. The developer needs not only a clear understanding of the algorithm's purpose, but also of the data being analyzed.

Inaccurate data. For example, an algorithm may use the electronic health record (EHR)'s problem list, either in plain language or through medical record coding, as part of its analysis. If the problem list is incomplete or out of date, or if the coding isn't correct, the conclusions of the algorithm will be inaccurate.

How should leaders identify and avert potential bias?

- AI staff should stay current with the research being devoted to addressing bias (see Box 8.1)
- Developers, whether internal staff or outside suppliers, should establish processes that mitigate bias (see Box 8.1)
- Human experts in the subject area should help developers interpret the data and check the conclusions of algorithms. For example, an expert in population health would notice that an algorithm failed to include the uninsured when identifying sick individuals.

Box 8.1   Fighting AI bias: research and tools

The science of fighting AI bias is evolving quickly. Some research resources include:

- The AI Now Institute's annual reports (https://ainowinstitute.org/)
- The Partnership on AI (https://www.partnershiponai.org/)
- The Alan Turing Institute's Fairness, Transparency, Privacy group (https://www.turing.ac.uk/)
- The Algorithmic Justice League (https://www.ajl.org/)

Bias mitigation practices and tools include:

- Google's Responsible AI Practices (https://ai.google/responsibilities/responsible-ai-practices/)
- IBM's AI Fairness 360 Framework (https://developer.ibm.com/technologies/artificial-intelligence/blogs/ai-fairness-360-attacking-bias-from-all-angles/)

8.3.3 Poor testing

Testing of an AI algorithm should proceed through three stages (Beam 2021). Problems can arise at each stage.

Stage 1: Designing and developing the model. During this stage, the model developer obtains a set of data that should represent data that the model will eventually use at scale. Some types of outcomes data may need to be annotated: a human must review it and explain to the algorithm what it's looking for.

The developer uses a subset of the data to train the model and create the first version of the model. Once the model has been developed, the rest of the data is used to test the model.

Stage 1 can be plagued by the biases in the data discussed earlier. In addition, the data can be "noisy" and difficult for the algorithm to understand because of variability in data annotation. For example, radiologists and/ or oncologists may review medical images and annotate whether an image shows a particular type of cancer. Even in real life, radiologists and oncologists often don't agree, and they may annotate the same image differently.

Stage 2: Prospective testing, using the model developed in Stage 1 to analyze live data. For example, a model developed on a set of data from a revenue cycle application is now tested on a new set of data from other revenue cycle applications and/or other institutions.

In Stage 2, the algorithm should encounter data that was not included in the training dataset. For example, the other revenue cycle applications may be from hospitals that had very large under-served populations or from regions that have different practice patterns from the institution in the training set. The model may see a significant performance degradation when it encounters these new situations, and will require adjustment to take them into account.

Stage 2 is supposed to determine whether the model works outside of the lab. Unfortunately, Stage 2 is all too often regarded as optional. A study by Topol (2019) reviewed dozens of published model results and found that only four included prospective testing. The remainder were based solely on Stage 1 training data.

Stage 3: Implementation. Once an algorithm is in use, it's easy to assume it's no longer in "testing," but because circumstances continually change, it must continue to be retrained with new data and tested. For example, moving from ICD-10 to ICD-11 could require a drastic overhaul of any algorithm that uses those diagnosis and billing codes. The increase in granularity from ICD-10's 14,000 codes to ICD-11's 55,000 codes, while potentially a dramatic improvement in the usefulness of the data, could cause catastrophic confusion to the existing algorithm.

Sometimes models need to be retrained in light of new data. Some tools—generally known as "MLOps" or "machine learning operations" solutions—can identify when models are no longer doing a good job of predicting, suggesting a need for retraining. Healthcare organizations should either have a MLOps process in place or ensure that their AI vendor has one.

How should healthcare organizations manage the training and testing process? Each stage should be documented, reviewed, conducted, and monitored by experienced personnel, focusing on the following questions:

Stage 1: Model training and development

- What data will be used for model development?
- Is the size of the database sufficient?
- What steps have been taken to ensure that the set of data represents the area that is the focus of the model?
- Is the data suitable for machine learning?
- What steps are taken to ensure that annotation is consistently and reliably performed?

Stage 2: Prospective testing

- Has prospective testing been performed?
- What data and settings were used for prospective testing?

Stage 3: Implementation

- What steps are taken to monitor changes in the data which might impact the model?
- Who is accountable for monitoring model performance over time and how do they carry out their responsibilities?

The organization must require detailed information about the testing process from every AI vendor that answers the questions above.

8.3.4 Lack of transparency

Machines "think" differently from humans. For example, AI algorithms can analyze images pixel by pixel. They may "see" the same cancerous lesions that a radiologist would, but have different criteria for identifying the lesions—criteria that are opaque to humans. An algorithm may be able to distinguish a photo of a dog from a photo of a cat, but its process for doing so may bear so little resemblance to our process that we can't understand it.

AI is complex and becoming more so, but when we apply it to health-care, we need to have some idea of how it works. It may not matter for a medical record coding application or an operating room scheduler, but an application that's helping identify disease or make patient care decisions should be explainable on some level. This concern is particularly relevant to complex deep learning models, which are difficult for even data scientists to understand (Davenport 2019).

Explainability as such doesn't always matter in healthcare. With or without AI, it's often not clear why a medication works for some patients and not others. We don't (yet) know why some heavy smokers live well into their 90s.

However, human clinicians must be prepared to explain their reasoning process, even though it may also be something of a "black box" combination of knowledge, experience, and intuition. In a similar sense, providers must have some way to validate the conclusions that the AI draws from the data. Every time the AI is correct, its success validates its process—whatever it is—but the (hopefully) growing pile of evidence doesn't preclude the need for monitoring and review.

To start with, providers need to trust the credibility of the developer and confirm that it uses good practices to ensure the integrity and fidelity of its models. These practices include those we discussed above in the sections on bias and testing.

In addition, healthcare organizations need to validate the data that underlies an AI algorithm. If it's their own data, they must make sure it's clean and in the form that the algorithm requires. If it comes from outside the organization, does it come from a trustworthy source? Can external and internal data be combined safely?

Clinicians should also know whether an AI product is "locked"—that is, it will always work the same way unless it is formally updated—or whether it is designed to learn and change as it acquires more data and gets feedback on its performance. Few models are retrained automatically and continuously; it is done episodically when humans provide new training data. Clinicians expect themselves and their colleagues to make better decisions as they learn and grow. Learning from new data over time is generally a desirable attribute for machine learning models as well, but clinicians must be aware of that attribute in their AI tools.

8.4   Regulatory risk

Healthcare AI applications may be classified as "medical devices" by the U.S. Food and Drug Administration (FDA). Before such devices can be used in clinical practice, they must be approved by the FDA or equivalent regulators in other countries. At the end of 2020, one review (Muehlematter 2021) showed that more than 220 AI-enabled "software as a medical device" applications had been approved by the FDA, and slightly more by European regulatory bodies, though only 124 applications had been approved in both the U.S.A. and Europe. Most approved devices involve either recognition of disease states from radiological images or classification of cardiological problems. Some are only software, but many are intended to function alongside MRI or CT machines, or in wearable devices like Apple watches.

The FDA has published guidelines for the regulation of artificial intelligence software as a medical device (Food and Drug Administration 2021a, 2021b). The FDA has a well-defined process for approving three different types of AI (new clinical pathway, substantially equivalent to an existing device, pre-market approval). However, inconsistencies in the FDA's requirements for testing and transparency have caused controversy and may continue to do so in the near future (Ross 2021b).

The FDA is examining how devices that leverage AI should be labeled. Such labeling is important for device transparency for consumers and practitioners, just as food labeling tells consumers what they are eating. It seems likely that the FDA will also eventually require some degree of algorithmic transparency in AI-related devices, both so that clinicians can interpret recommendations or predictions for patients, and so that any algorithmic bias can be detected.

To address the "learning" aspect of AI, the FDA will examine the manufacturer's Algorithm Change Protocol (ACP), which explains how the manufacturer proposes that the algorithm will learn and change while remaining safe and effective.

The FDA also understands that AI algorithms may have bias (see above) and will explore regulatory approaches to ensuring the robustness and resilience of these algorithms to withstand changing clinical inputs and conditions. The FDA regulation will apply to AI involved with provision of care, but not to administrative uses.

Coordination of regulatory requirements would be helpful for both developers and customers. Three regulatory agencies—the U.S. FDA, Health Canada, and the U.K. Medicine and Health Products Regulatory Agency (MHRA)—have issued a joint statement of ten principles for developing AI-enabled healthcare applications, based on the application of good manufacturing practices to software development:

1. Multi-disciplinary expertise is leveraged throughout the total product life cycle.
2. Good software engineering and security practices are implemented.
3. Clinical study participants and datasets are representative of the intended patient population.
4. Training datasets are independent of test sets.
5. Selected reference datasets are based upon best available methods.
6. Model design is tailored to the available data and reflects the intended use of the device.
7. Focus is placed on the performance of the Human–AI team: Where the model has a "human in the loop," human factors considerations and the human interpretability of the model outputs are addressed with emphasis on the performance of the Human–AI team, rather than just the performance of the model in isolation.

8. Testing demonstrates device performance during clinically relevant conditions.
9. Users are provided clear, essential information including: the product's intended use and indications for use, performance of the model for appropriate subgroups, characteristics of the data used to train and test the model, acceptable inputs, known limitations, user interface interpretation, and clinical workflow integration of the model.
10. Deployed models are monitored for performance and retraining risks are managed (FDA 2021b).

We can expect that all countries will eventually have some form of regulation for AI software as a medical device. However, at this writing, the regulatory environment for health-related AI is a moving target. Organizations moving to incorporate AI into healthcare delivery should make themselves aware of the current status of regulation, both in general and as it pertains to the particular tech being considered.

8.5   Liability and malpractice risk

If harm results from a clinician using an AI-enabled application, who is liable? A thorough discussion of this issue is beyond the scope of this book, and the legal answers will vary among jurisdictions. The legal landscape, like everything else about AI, is evolving rapidly (Sullivan 2019). Can AI developers be liable for harm that occurred because their product behaved in ways they couldn't anticipate? Should an AI be considered a "person" for the purposes of allocating liability? Should a physician be required to understand how an AI functions in order to rely on its recommendations—even though its own creators may not understand it?

Even in a period of rapid change, we can identify several ways that use of AI might affect liability:

Control: Depending on how AI fits into the workflow, the responsibility for clinical decisions can become fuzzy. To take an example from another realm, if a manufacturer makes a self-driving car and doesn't allow the driver to intervene, then the manufacturer, or perhaps the designer of the algorithm, may be liable for any injuries, rather than the driver (who is just a passenger). But when the AI is assisting the driver, responsibility still accrues to a driver who accepts a clearly unwise suggestion (or rejects a clearly wise one).

In the context of healthcare, the "driver" could be held responsible for deciding to cede control to the "car" in the first place: for example, a radiologist who depends on AI to make the first pass at an imaging study that might contain thousands of images and pick out 100 that it thinks might show an abnormality. If the algorithm misses one, the trust that the physician places in it might end up harming a patient.

On the other hand, it seems clear that AI will eventually become the standard of care for reading images, at least as a "second set of eyes." Once that happens, radiologists who miss a malignancy could be held liable for *not* giving AI the first or second pass. Mammograms were once new and the standard of care was a manual breast exam, but now that mammography is the standard of care, no physician would recommend skipping a mammogram in favor of a manual exam.

Dependence: Virtually everyone has had occasion to regret an over-reliance on spellcheck or autocorrect, which is among the simplest forms of AI in common use. Likewise, errors can easily sneak into the electronic health record if an aggressive AI records the wrong drug, a sound-alike diagnosis, or a note that the clinician performed some routine action that was not performed in that particular case. Many organizations have successfully battled cut-and-paste syndrome in their EHRs, but they may have to redouble their efforts to fight AI-enabled autofill and keep clinicians vigilant.

AI algorithms may give clinicians a false sense of security. For example, an algorithm (such as the one described earlier in this chapter that's embedded into the Epic EHR) might promise to flag patients who are at risk for sepsis, based on patterns in their vital signs, before physicians or nurses might notice. If clinicians relax their guard because they are depending on the algorithm to generate an alarm, they are still responsible if a sepsis crisis occurs on their watch.

Disclosure: Liability for using many types of medical treatments, from devices to diagnostics to drugs, often relies on the concept of the "learned intermediary." If the manufacturer fully discloses all information to the clinician, it falls on the clinician to evaluate that information and deter-

Table 8.1   Examples of potential legal outcomes related to AI use in clinical practice

Scenario	AI recommendation	AI accuracy	Physician action	Patient outcome	Legal outcome (probable)
1	Standard of care	Correct	Follows	Good	No injury and no liability
2	Standard of care	Correct	Rejects	Bad	Injury and liability
3	Standard of care	Incorrect (standard of care is incorrect)	Follows	Bad	Injury and no liability
4	Standard of care	Incorrect (standard of care is incorrect)	Rejects	Good	No injury and no liability
5	Nonstandard care	Correct (standard of care is incorrect)	Follows	Good	No injury and no liability
6	Nonstandard care	Correct (standard of care is incorrect)	Rejects	Bad	Injury and no liability
7	Nonstandard care	Incorrect	Follows	Bad	Injury and liability
8	Nonstandard care	Incorrect	Rejects	Good	No injury and no liability

Source: Price 2019.

mine whether the use of that drug or diagnostic is appropriate and worth any risks that it poses.

The same principle applies to AI algorithms, and a wise vendor will provide risk and disclaimer information as comprehensive as the terrifying information inserts that come with a typical medication. Clinicians can protect themselves to some extent by passing all that information to the patient and carefully going over it with them. If the vendor shares clinical results showing that their product's diagnoses or treatment recommendations were accurate in 85 percent of cases, the patient can use that information in evaluating the proposed course of treatment.

Table 8.1 demonstrates how different scenarios for using AI might affect a physician's liability. When there is injury, the determination of liability may rest on the combination of whether the AI recommended an accepted standard of care, and whether the physician followed the recommendation.

Healthcare organizations should not let the risks we've described prevent them from exploring the astonishing potential of AI, but they must be aware and give them adequate weight in their decision process. In the next chapter we will discuss how to minimize them through managing your AI adoption process effectively.

References

Beam, A. (2021). Understanding the AI development pipeline. Presentation made to the Leading Digital Transformation in Health Care program, Harvard Medical School Executive Education, May 26.

Buolamwini, J. and Gebru, T. (2018). Gender shades: intersectional accuracy disparities in commercial gender classification. *Proceedings of Machine Learning Research* 81: 1–15. Conference on Fairness, Accountability, and Transparency, 2018. http://proceedings.mlr.press/v81/buolamwini18a/buolamwini18a.pdf.

Dastin, J. (2018). Amazon scraps secret AI recruiting tool that showed bias against women. *Reuters*, October 10. https://www.reuters.com/article/us-amazon-com-jobs-automation-insight/amazon-scraps-secret-ai-recruiting-tool-that-showed-bias-against-women-idUSKCN1MK08G.

Davenport, T. and Kalakota, R. (2019). The potential for artificial intelligence in healthcare. *Future Healthcare Journal*, 6(2): 94–8. http://doi.org/10.7861/futurehosp.6-2-94.

Davenport, T., Redman, T. and Godfrey, B. (2020). To fight pandemics, we need better data. *MIT Sloan Management Review*, August 24. https://shop .sloanreview.mit.edu/store/to-fight-pandemics-we-need-better-data.

Food and Drug Administration (2021a). Artificial Intelligence/Machine Learning (AI/ML)-based software as a medical device (SaMD) action plan. https://www .fda.gov/media/145022/download.

Food and Drug Administration (2021b). Good machine learning practice for medical device development: guiding principles. https://www.fda.gov/medical -devices/software-medical-device-samd/good-machine-learning-practice -medical-device-development-guiding-principles.

Heaven, D. (2019). Why deep-learning AIs are so easy to fool. *Nature* news feature, October 11. https://www.nature.com/articles/d41586-019-03013-5.

Lohr, S. (2021). What ever happened to IBM's Watson? *New York Times*, July 16.   https://www.nytimes.com/2021/07/16/technology/what-happened-ibm -watson.html.

Muehlematter, U.J., Daniore, P. and Vokinger, K.N. (2021). Approval of artificial intelligence and machine learning-based medical devices in the USA and Europe (2015–20): a comparative analysis. *Lancet Digital Health*, 3(3): e195–e203. https://www.thelancet.com/journals/landig/article/PIIS2589-7500(20)30292 -2/fulltext.

Obermeyer, Z., Powers, B., Vogeli, C. and Mullainathan, S. (2019). Dissecting racial bias in an algorithm used to manage the health of populations. *Science*, 366(6464): 447–53. http://doi.org/10.1126/science.aax2342.

Pratt, M. (2020). Machine learning bias (AI bias). TechTarget/SearchEnterpriseAI. https://searchenterpriseai.techtarget.com/definition/machine-learning-bias -algorithm-bias-or-AI-bias.

Price, W.N. II, Gerke, S. and Cohen, I.G. (2019). Potential liability for physicians using artificial intelligence. *JAMA*, 322(18): 1765–6. http://doi.org/10.1001/ jama.2019.15064.

Roberts, M., Driggs, D., Thorpe, M., et al. (2021). Common pitfalls and rec-ommendations for using machine learning to detect and prognosticate for COVID-19 using chest radiographs and CT scans. *Nature Machine Intelligence*, 3: 199–217. https://doi.org/10.1038/s42256-021-00307-0.

Ross, C. and Aguilar, M. (2021a). Inside the fall of Watson Health: how IBM's audacious plan to 'change the face of health care' with AI fell apart. *STAT News*, March 8. https://www.statnews.com/2021/03/08/ibm-watson-health-sale/.

Ross, C. (2021b). As the FDA clears a flood of AI tools, missing data raise trou-bling questions on safety and fairness. *STAT News*, February 3. https://www .statnews.com/2021/02/03/fda-clearances-artificial-intelligence-data/.

Ross, C. (2021c). Epic's sepsis algorithm is going off the rails in the real world: the use of these variables may explain why. *STAT News*, September 27. https://www .statnews.com/2021/09/27/epic-sepsis-algorithm-antibiotics-model/.

Ross, C. (2021d). Machine learning is booming in medicine: it's also facing a credibility crisis. *STAT News*, June 2. https://www.statnews.com/2021/06/02/ machine-learning-ai-methodology-research-flaws/.

Strickland, E. (2019). How IBM Watson overpromised and underdelivered on AI health care. *IEEE Spectrum*, April 2. https://spectrum.ieee.org/how-ibm -watson-overpromised-and-underdelivered-on-ai-health-care.

Sullivan, H.R. and Schweikart, S.J. (2019). Are current tort liability doctrines adequate for addressing injury caused by AI? *AMA Journal of Ethics*, 21(2): E160–E166. https://journalofethics.ama-assn.org/article/are-current-tort-liability-doctrines-adequate-addressing-injury-caused-ai/2019-02?utm_effort=0.

Topol, E. (2019). High-performance medicine: the convergence of human and AI. *Nature Medicine*, 25(1): 44. https://www.nature.com/articles/s41591-018-0300-7.

Wong, A., Otles, E., Donnelly, J.P., et al. (2021). External validation of a widely implemented proprietary sepsis prediction model in hospitalized patients. *JAMA Internal Medicine*, 181(8): 1065–70. http://doi.org/10.1001/jamainternmed.2021.2626.

Wynants, L., et al. (2020). Prediction models for diagnosis and prognosis of Covid-19: systematic review and critical appraisal. *British Medical Journal*, 369: m1328. http://dx.doi.org/10.1136/bmj.m1328.

9 Moving forward: how to integrate AI into your organization

9.1 Introduction

Introducing AI into the operation of a healthcare organization raises issues that won't manage themselves, no matter how smart the AI is. An organization's leaders—and not just those in IT—need to understand AI technologies, how they can be used to support their organization's strategy and operations, and how they can be misused. There's no substitute for their (your) involvement, and that's why we've written this book and particularly this chapter.

9.2 AI management contexts

As an executive of a healthcare provider organization, you'll usually be managing AI in one of three broad contexts:

Micro: You're considering acquiring a product or service that claims to be "AI-based" or to use AI to substantially enhance the product's performance. Will it improve what you're doing? Are there risks you need to understand? Is it a good way to try out AI before making a larger commitment?

Meso: You've already made that larger commitment and are implementing AI across several different functions of the organization. How do you develop an AI-enabled portfolio of capabilities, and how do you reap the benefits of those new capabilities to achieve your goals?

Macro: You've realized that AI can help you become a data-driven, learning healthcare organization, which you must do to thrive under the data-driven, value-based payment models that your payers are adopting. How can you structure your adoption of AI to fundamentally transform how you operate?

9.2.1   Micro: evaluating the AI sales pitch

Healthcare organizations won't often buy AI—as such—on its own. If they do, it will probably be as an experimental tool, rather than a "production" application. It's far more likely that production deployments of AI will be integrated into other products or services: an MRI machine, a building control system, a utilization management application. Customers don't need to understand the guts of how AI works, any more than they need to understand how a cell tower works to take a call in their car. But they do need to ask some questions of the vendor to understand how it's going to help them and what challenges they will face in implementation.

Here are a few to start with:

How are you applying AI in your products? What can your products do, as a result, that they couldn't do before, and why do I want that? (Those same questions can be used with any vendor, whether it's MRI or building control systems.)

How have you tested these capabilities? What were the results? Do we have to change our processes or our organization to achieve comparable results, and if so, how?

Where do you get the content that your AI is based on? How do you keep your algorithms and your predictions current? How often do you update as the world changes? If the AI is based on machine learning, what are the sources of data used to train the algorithms? How do you ensure that the data has minimal bias?

Is there anything special that I need to teach my staff? Will the application interface change routinely? Will the product behave in ways that they don't expect? How does the product fit into their workflow? How will the product change as it "learns"?

How am I protected if your AI makes a mistake? What are the liability provisions in your contract?

Of course, you will also ask the questions you usually ask during the selection of any major product or service. For example, how much does the product cost? Who else has used it and what has been their experience?

If you do acquire or build some AI capabilities as an experiment, pilot project, or "proof of concept," keep in mind that many such projects are never deployed into production. Some surveys have found, for example, that almost 90 percent of machine learning models are never deployed (Davenport 2020). The result is, of course, no economic or organizational value. There is nothing wrong with experimenting on a small scale, but organizations should plan to move the system into production if it meets all the salient criteria created for the experiment.

9.2.2   Meso: integrating AI into a spectrum of operations

AI, like other innovative tech, often finds its way into a department through an interested champion or super-user. The same is true at the system level. Perhaps a board member says, "We need to be aggressively pursuing AI! I heard that our rival health system is working closely with Tech Giant, Inc., and if we are not careful, we will be out of business!"

It's all too easy to rush in, but there are more failed AI implementations than successful ones. Hasty decisions can waste money and time, divert the organization from its goals, and allow more disciplined competitors to eat the organization's lunch with wiser technology choices and better implementation.

The AI application that caught the board member's eye might make recommendations that enrage the medical staff—or worse, mystify them. The well-publicized problems encountered by MD Anderson Cancer Center with IBM's Watson ($62 million spent with little to show for it) illustrate the chasm that can form between the marketing hype of AI and the clinical reality of its attempted use (Strickland 2019). Watson for Oncology used natural language processing (NLP) and other techniques to examine hundreds of variables—including demographics, tumor characteristics, treatments, and outcomes—and developed diagnosis and treatment recommendations. However, Watson did not "think" like an oncologist and many of the recommendations were wrong or trivial. Oncologists learned not to trust the system.

Sometimes what sounds like a good idea is a bad idea. Sometimes even if the tech is ready, your organization may not be. Sometimes an AI idea is a good idea but not as good as some non-AI ideas. No matter how flashy or potentially revolutionary, successful AI implementation requires the same boring due diligence and hard work as any other organizational investment.

How do you assess a smorgasbord of AI investment opportunities and develop a network of stable, healthy AI initiatives that make up an important foundation for the organization's digital transformation? How do you avoid AI initiatives that will leave the organization fodder for a case study in what not to do?

Step 1: Focus on the business goals. AI is only valuable to the extent that it can be effectively applied to achieve organizational goals. Suppose your organization has embraced two goals: becoming an insurer as well as a provider of care (leveraging both to advance care quality and efficiency); and providing an outstanding service and care experience for patients. Being both a provider and a payer changes a health system's economic equation. Because it's billing itself for the care it provides, any technology must help the organization deliver both better care and lower cost. And to provide an outstanding experience, its push for efficiency must also include personalization to keep patients from feeling like they're getting cookie-cutter care.

Step 2: Understand how AI might further those business goals. You should be able to state in one or two sentences how AI can address these two goals. For example, applying AI to electronic health record (EHR) data may enable you to identify the best treatment quickly. Your call center could use AI-based bots, trained to recognize emotions and cultural expressions, to personalize its responses to patients who have questions about their health or recent insurance bills.

Table 9.1   Current AI priorities for healthcare organizations

	Hospitals	Health Plans	Life Sciences	Employers
Priority 1	Improve reimbursement coding (45%)	Improve reimbursement coding (40%)	Accelerate research (47%)	Monitor Internet of Things data (47%)
Priority 2	Monitor Internet of Things data (38%)	Automate administrative processes (40%)	Identify patients for trials (44%)	Accelerate research (45%)
Priority 3	Accelerate research (36%)	Detect fraud, waste, and abuse (39%)	Enable personalized communications (39%)	Enable personalized communications/ Automate administrative processes (35% each)

Source: Optum 2020.

The statement of capabilities helps leadership understand the full range of potential uses: for example, recognizing patterns in data such as conversational voice, analyzing radiology images, and tracking medication-purchasing patterns to flag disease outbreaks and potential medication side effects. A truly potent technology will spread well beyond its initial application.

An early and (by today's standards) crude iteration of AI featured in most EHRs—clinical decision support (CDS)—sends clinicians suggestions and reminders, and flags relevant recent research based on the information in the patient's record. While CDS can drive a clinician up the wall with too many alerts, a properly deployed system can transform care. For example, many hospitals sharply reduced the number of patients who developed pneumonia while on a ventilator by adopting a bundle of standard practices to prevent infection and using their CDS to remind clinicians to use those practices.

Table 9.1 provides the results of a survey on the priorities for AI implementation for a sample of hospitals, health plans, life sciences firms, and employers.

Step 3: Expect obstacles and prepare for iterative learning. New technologies can sometimes show up dings, dents, and dirt in their surroundings. For example, as you apply your newly acquired AI capability to identify treatment effectiveness, you may have to finally face up to and deal with the uneven (or even outright poor) quality of your EHR data. Maybe your physicians have been relying on the "notes" field instead of checking the boxes. Maybe key pieces of data end up in the wrong fields or are not documented at all. Understanding and fixing these issues is crucial to reap the full benefits of your new AI—or possibly to get it to function at all.

Sometimes technical and workflow issues get in the way. For example, Heaven (2020) describes an AI-based application that was to be used to screen for diabetic retinopathy. A trial of the technology in a hospital in Thailand ran into multiple problems. Poor quality of photos of the eye led to images being rejected and patients being told that they'd have to visit another specialist at another clinic on another day. Poor internet connections often delayed AI-based interpretation for hours.

The most transformative technologies usually take a while, and require several iterations, to demonstrate their value, stabilize the technology, and implement the change management steps needed to achieve that value. You might need to improve data quality, expand the scope of data captured, alter existing workflows, provide education to clinicians and/or improve the performance of the AI algorithms.

9.2.3   Macro: becoming a data-driven organization

In a data-driven organization, important decisions are informed by data and analytics and managers and clinicians act on analytically derived insights rather than intuition or experience (Davenport 2020). In these organizations, the contribution of data to organizational performance is broad and deep. The organization uses data to drive innovation and competes on data and analytics. This focus on data creates a learning health system, in which knowledge-generating processes, embedded into daily practice, produce continual improvement in care (National Academy of Medicine 2007).

Most healthcare organizations have not been predominantly data-driven; particularly in clinical matters they are more likely driven by the intuition and experience of their clinicians. Evidence-based care innovations frequently take years to achieve wide adoption when they challenge that intuition and experience. Transforming the fundamental nature of an organization is exceptionally difficult (Bean 2021). The impedi-

Table 9.2   Status of progress in becoming a data-driven organization

Contribution of data strategy	Percentage of respondents performing
Driving innovation with data	48
Competing on analytics	41
Have a well-articulated data strategy	30
Experiencing transformational business outcomes	29
Have forged a data culture	24
Created a data-driven organization	24

Source: New Vantage Partners 2021.

ments include cultural challenges, redesigning core business processes, acquiring necessary skills and retraining existing managers and staff, and revamping reward systems.

AI is an important tool in advancing an organization's efforts to become more data-driven, by enabling deeper insights into the data and connecting the dots in a host of new ways. But adding AI will not make the transformation any easier and might make it harder. AI techniques can be mysterious to clinicians and staff. Everyone in the organization must trust the AI, and that means that the AI must be trustworthy. Glitchy technology or clearly biased results can undermine trust and derail the implementation.

A progress report by New Vantage Partners (2021) found the following in a multi-industry survey of the status of corporate data-driven initiatives— many of them in large and sophisticated companies. As Table 9.2 shows, becoming a data-driven organization is a work in progress.

The following sections discuss in more detail the changes that health systems will have to make to embrace AI as an integral component of a broad spectrum of organizational activities and part of their transformation into data-driven organizations—the meso and macro contexts.

9.3   Organizing for AI

Regardless of your stage of AI adoption, several capabilities of your organization can greatly affect your ability—for better or for worse—to use it effectively. In this section, we discuss several areas where you'll need to examine and possibly overhaul how things work today. Prowess in these capabilities will occur faster and more effectively in organizations that declare AI adoption to be a strategic priority than in organizations that view it as a novelty or niche technology.

9.3.1   Governance

Adoption of AI at scale raises new, sometimes utterly unfamiliar, governance issues. Organizations must strike a balance: supporting innovation, developing controls that reduce risk, maintaining efficiency, instilling organizational learning, and ensuring that the portfolio is well executed.

We suggest that these governance tasks fall to a committee composed of organizational leaders, including the Chief Information Officer, Chief Financial Officer, Chief Medical Officer, Chief Legal Officer, Chief Nursing Officer, physician leadership, Chief Academic Officer, and board members. This committee would:

- Manage the processes that generate a portfolio of AI initiatives
- Address issues and challenges related to AI data, implementation, and use
- Develop and manage relationships with AI product and service suppliers
- Ensure the development of a digital architecture that integrates AI capabilities into the organization's applications and infrastructure
- Develop an approach to teaching the organization about the power and limitations of AI
- Monitor AI applications for ethical and regulatory issues

This governance structure may be temporary. When new powerful technologies emerge, healthcare organizations often form governance structures that help them learn about a technology and develop mature approaches to its ongoing use: for example, the Internet in the 1990s and tablet and phone apps in the early 2000s. These committees are disbanded once the technology becomes a well-understood and integral component of the organization's strategy and operations.

9.3.2 Innovation management

To create and sustain an environment friendly to effective AI use, an organization needs a person, a unit, or a department (depending on the size of the organization) to guide the adoption of AI across the organization.

As we discussed earlier, larger health systems and organizations may decide to establish a formal AI Center of Excellence (Davenport 2019), staffed by data scientists, workflow analysts, and change management specialists who work with the clinical and business leadership to drive the effective adoption of AI.

A center can report to one of several health system leaders, but most commonly reports to the Chief Information Officer or the Chief Digital Officer. Some healthcare organizations may also establish Chief Analytics Officer or Chief Data and Analytics Officer roles. The center could be combined with an existing analytics group and have the same reporting relationship. Most of the staff members in the center should have a dotted line relationship to a business unit such as Finance, Nursing, or Research Administration. Those relationships enable the center to develop a solid understanding of the needs and culture of those units and improve its ability to respond to their needs.

Regardless of its form, the innovation management function has several responsibilities:

Work with leadership to develop the vision for AI for the organization. What is AI? What can it do? How might it enable new business models and strategies?

Identify business-driven use cases. A prioritized set of pilots and deployments at scale must strike a balance across the needs of various stakeholders, and between low- and high-risk projects. Each requires consideration of related process changes, project goals, and effective project management.

Determine the appropriate level of ambition. Significant AI-driven advances are rarely accomplished in one project or initiative. Each project builds on the ones that came before it and provides a foundation for those that come after. The innovation management function needs to develop project roadmaps to keep the organization focused on its goals. An AI-based revenue cycle initiative, for example, might start with using AI to extract the data from the various types of documents—PDFs, faxes, paper bills, etc.—used to communicate with payers and patients. Several projects may be needed, each targeted to extracting a particular type of data and using AI to reconcile that data with other data.

Create a target data and technical architecture. AI initiatives and implementations require a data and technical architecture that may go beyond what the organization currently supports. The innovation management function can define the scope of data needed for a particular AI application (e.g., data from wearable devices, genetic tests, and social determinants of health), the sources and standards for that data, and the analytics, data management, and workflow integration tools needed. This process will include determining the approaches to integrate the AI tools that are part of applications such as electronic health records and population health management systems.

Develop and maintain a network of AI champions. A network of administrative and clinical champions across the health system can help provide political and budget support and identify promising initiatives.

Spread success stories. Highlighting "wins" from any new technology helps with political support for it, which may be particularly important for a transformative technology like AI. The success stories can illustrate how to leverage AI technology and may spark further innovation throughout the organization.

Monitor the evolution of the technology. Keeping up with the pace of AI development is challenging but necessary. The center staff can leverage access to consultants, vendors, conferences, their counterparts in other organizations and publications to gather and interpret industry progress. This monitoring will complement information and insight gathering by other members of the organization through their professional connections.

Ensure the successful transition of AI pilots to implementation at scale.
Once a pilot of an AI application has been completed, the organization
may decide to implement that application across the enterprise. The
center staff may not lead the implementation, but they can provide
guidance. Organizations will adopt AI more quickly and smoothly if they
already know how to move new technologies from pilot to broad deployment and manage the accompanying workflow and/or cultural changes.

9.3.3   Talent management

The demand for AI and data science talent is significant, and outstrips
the growth of the general labor market and even of other IT-related positions. The U.S. Bureau of Labor Statistics projects a 22 percent growth for
data science positions between 2020 and 2030. In contrast, all computer
occupations combined are expected to grow by 13 percent in that time
and the overall job growth rate is projected at 8 percent (Bureau of Labor
Statistics 2021).

Research-oriented organizations will have an easier time with recruit-
ment. Others will need to innovate. For example:

- Develop relationships with local data science college or university
  programs, including providing internship opportunities and adjunct
  faculty to teach in these programs
- Identify companies that can provide contract data science talent
- Leverage the data science skills of healthcare application vendors,
  e.g., Cerner and Epic, and technology firms such as Google, IBM,
  Microsoft, and Amazon
- Develop internal training programs to "grow your own."

Even if you don't have a large in-house AI capability, your vendors
should. When acquiring an AI-based product or service, ask the vendor
about their approach to obtaining and retaining the needed talent.

9.3.4   Data management

In an era of value-based care, healthcare organizations can use AI-based
tools to understand their care cost, quality, and safety. They can assess
their competitive position and their patients' satisfaction. However, as
they implement these tools, organizations invariably encounter problems
with their data: gaps and inconsistencies, insufficient scope (e.g., lack of

data on social determinants), and murky definitions. The limited inter-operability in healthcare exacerbates these problems, as does the need to balance EHR usability and structured data capture. While drop-down menus and checkboxes produce AI-friendly data, they alienate clinicians who just want to dash off a quick note in a free-text box.

Organizations don't have to be trying to implement AI to be hampered by poor quality data, of course, but bad data can completely derail an AI project. There has been some progress in using AI itself to achieve better data management: for example, by integrating overlapping databases or using AI to resolve inconsistencies in the data.

However, data management, and the oversight function called data governance, is still mostly a time-consuming, exacting, and often tedious human responsibility. It involves the creation and ongoing management of the organization structures, policies, and processes needed to define, control, and ensure the quality of the data. Data governance functions include:

- Define "how" the organization will manage its data and the policies, procedures, technologies, and tools needed to facilitate this process
- Outline the steps and tools necessary for making changes to the list of strategic data elements and their definitions
- Describe the processes for identifying, capturing, and managing new types of data, e.g., data from wearable devices
- Define the roles and responsibilities for managing the organization's data asset
- Prioritize the demand for analyses and ensure that unmet demand does not lead to problems such as the creation of shadow systems
- Understand data regulations, e.g., privacy and quality reporting, and ensuring compliance with those regulations.

9.3.5   Technology architecture

As we've discussed, AI is almost always part of something else: patient wearable devices, building environmental controls, EHRs, MRIs and CT scanners, chatbots, and revenue cycle applications.

If the AI is self-contained within an application or device and is well supported by the supplier, then the organization doesn't have to worry too much about how it works, though it's good to have some idea. But if the organization has substantial responsibility for supplying the AI application with data, determining exactly what it does with that data, and ensuring that the AI application is well integrated into clinician workflow, then it must consider the technology architecture that supports the application. The most relevant aspects are the "layers" above and below the AI logic and processing engine.

The layer below is the data used by the AI logic. As discussed above, strong data management is needed to supply the AI logic with data that's consistently defined and collected.

Primarily for business and competitive reasons (rather than technical ones), interoperability among healthcare software applications has ranged from weak to nonexistent, and technology architecture discussions all too often revolve around how to induce the applications to talk among themselves using an array of interfaces. That situation is changing, thanks to market pressures and the U.S. federal government's recent adoption of interoperability requirements for healthcare applications (ONC 2020). Other countries are expected to implement the same requirements.

The federal effort has focused on requiring EHRs and health plan applications to support standardized application programming interfaces (APIs) based on the Fast Healthcare Interoperability Resources (FHIR, pronounced "fire") standards. The central goal is to develop applications that support consumer and patient management of their health and healthcare; the APIs enable these applications to read and write EHR data. AI-based apps can also use these APIs to "sit on top" of and access EHR data.

For example, an AI algorithm to predict the likelihood of hospitalization could use these APIs to read, from the EHR, a patient's diagnoses, recent lab results and co-morbidities. It could also pull data from sensors and monitoring devices the patient might be using at home, such as a "smart" pacemaker or glucose meter or a Wi-Fi-enabled scale. The algorithm could then calculate the patient's risk of a hospitalization and give a patient (and/or the patient's care team) a warning if it looks like they're at risk for a crisis. It could also recommend measures to prevent the crisis.

The layer above is the applications that use the output of the AI prediction (for example, whatever application alerts clinicians of the impending crisis described above). Sometimes the use of the output is straightforward. But, in other cases the architecture must enable the integration of the AI output into the application workflow such as using an EHR. This integration can be particularly challenging when there are a multitude of niche AI applications to be integrated.

AI platforms. The architecture will need to consider the potential utility of AI platforms. A platform is a group of technologies used as a base for other applications, processes, or technologies. You might hear of a Windows platform or web-based platform. Facebook is a platform that supports communities and individuals sharing with each other.

For a particular domain (e.g., radiology) there will be dozens of AI algorithms. The algorithms could plug into an AI platform using FHIR APIs; the platform then connects to one or more EHRs. This avoids the need for each algorithm to implement a connection to each EHR and can provide the clinician with a single algorithm interface.

The AI platform can also be used to aggregate the output of AI algorithms such that there is one "mailbox" used by all the algorithms. This aggregation could ease the challenge of workflow integration.

A "home" for AI output. The architecture may also need to resolve conflicts among competing AI application capabilities and determine a "home" for the output.

For example, managing the health of populations requires creating care plans for individual patients (Glaser 2020a). These plans consider patient status and health goals, and the plans dynamically respond to changes in patient condition. AI is an important foundation for these plans.

Should these intelligent plan capabilities be part of the EHR, the population health management application, or a person's personal health record? Or all of these? If changes are made in one place, how do they propagate to the others? The architecture discussion attempts to resolve this collision of capabilities.

Organizations that have deployed core transaction applications, such as EHRs and revenue cycle applications, will be better positioned to incorporate AI into the workflow. In addition, that incorporation will be simpler and faster in organizations that have a base of applications from one vendor across the enterprise than those with applications from multiple vendors.

9.4   Implementation risk management

AI projects face the same risks as any other IT venture, whether pilots or implementations at scale. Failure may be a spectacular collapse or merely overrun budgets, blown timetables, and incomplete achievement of project goals. If change management is weak—if the organization fails to create a sense of urgency, or if changes are introduced too quickly or too slowly—projects can fail from lack of momentum or from overwhelming the staff.

These IT implementation risks may afflict your AI initiatives:

• The technology is not well integrated into the workflow
• The use of the technology is cumbersome and time-consuming, and staff quickly give up
• The rationale for introducing the new technology is murky or not explained well, and users feel like they're being asked to change for no good reason
• Governance of the implementation is confusing, changes direction frequently, and doesn't include all stakeholders.

In addition, AI initiatives can have unique risk factors. Joshi et al. (2021) cite several:

The hammer in search of a nail. The AI initiative may involve elegant and impressively accurate algorithms that nonetheless don't address a problem that the organization cares about. Project proponents fall in love with the tech and ignore its irrelevance. It is a basic refrain that bears repeating from time to time—AI (and indeed all IT initiatives) needs to be driven by a business problem or opportunity.

Right solution, wrong time. The AI initiative may be addressing an important business issue, but the timing is not right to scale the initiative. Timing problems can result from shifts in priorities attributed to multiple factors; pandemics, changes in senior leadership, shifts in competitive dynamics, and new regulations.

Right tool, wrong user. The AI initiative may be a terrific way to address an issue, but the expected users are not the right users. For example, a predictive algorithm that identifies individuals at risk of deterioration in their chronic condition may be initially directed to informing the patient's physician. However, care managers may be in the best position to act on the recommendations.

To mitigate or remove these risks, start by answering these questions:

- What problems are we solving?
- Is the timing right for implementation at scale?
- Do we understand the best users of the AI innovation?
- Do we have people who know how to implement in charge of the implementation?
- Have we established mechanisms to provide ongoing oversight of model performance so that we can detect bias and deterioration?
- Have we applied "good manufacturing practices" to model and application development and implementation so that we can minimize the likelihood that professional negligence leads to liability problems?
- Does our contract reflect the most current thinking on how to allocate liability if harm results from the AI application, and does it protect us adequately?

9.5   In conclusion

Artificial intelligence has the potential to be an exceptionally powerful tool in our collective efforts to transform healthcare. We've illustrated this potential in our opening scenario in the preface and our review of current and emerging AI applications across a wider range of uses in patient care, care operations, personal health management, and the creation of new health devices and pharmaceuticals.

The value of a new technology is not automatic. There is no technology genie who waves her wand and—shazam!—an organization or an industry is transformed. The value of technology happens when it is managed to happen, and AI is no exception.

This book should help you—professionals who lead healthcare organizations—to manage the creation of value from AI. We've provided an overview of AI technologies and given multiple examples of its use. We've examined the potential impact of AI on the healthcare workforce and discussed regulatory, liability, and algorithm risks and challenges that will accompany the technology. We've shared approaches that organizations can take to ensure that the implementation of AI is thoughtful, goal-directed, and effective.

Leveraging AI to improve health and healthcare will be a long and challenging journey. This has been true for all profound technologies. Those who lead this journey will make healthcare safer, more efficient, of higher quality, and more accessible to their families, friends, and communities.

It is a journey worth making.[1]

Note

1. An earlier version of section 9.2.2 first appeared in J. Glaser (2020b), "When should health systems invest in new tech?" *Harvard Business Review*, November 12. The version is reused with permission.

References

Bean, R. (2021). Why is it so hard to become a data-driven company? *Harvard Business Review*, February. https://hbr.org/2021/02/why-is-it-so-hard-to-become-a-data-driven-company.

Bureau of Labor Statistics (2021). Occupational outlook handbook. U.S. Department of Labor. https://www.bls.gov/ooh/computer-and-information-technology/computer-and-information-research-scientists.htm#tab-1.

Davenport, T. and Dasgupta, S. (2019). How to set up an AI center of excellence. *Harvard Business Review*, January. https://hbr.org/2019/01/how-to-set-up-an-ai-center-of-excellence.

Davenport, T. and Mittal, N. (2020). How CEOs can lead a data-driven culture. *Harvard Business Review*, March 23. https://hbr.org/2020/03/how-ceos-can-lead-a-data-driven-culture.

Glaser, J. (2020a). It's time for a new kind of electronic health record. *Harvard Business Review*, June 12. https://hbr.org/2020/06/its-time-for-a-new-kind-of-electronic-health-record.

Glaser, J. (2020b). When should health systems invest in new tech? *Harvard Business Review*, November 12. https://hbr.org/2020/11/when-should-health-systems-invest-in-new-tech.

Heaven, W. (2020). Google's medical AI was super accurate in a lab: real life was a different story. *MIT Technology Review*, April 27. https://www.technologyreview.com/2020/04/27/1000658/google-medical-ai-accurate-lab-real-life-clinic-covid-diabetes-retina-disease/.

Joshi, M., Su, N., Austin, R. and Sundaram, A. (2021). Why so many data science projects fail to deliver. *Sloan Management Review*, March. https://sloanreview.mit.edu/article/why-so-many-data-science-projects-fail-to-deliver/.

National Academy of Medicine (2007). *The Learning Healthcare System*. Washington, D.C.: National Academies Press.

New Vantage Partners (2021). *Big Data and AI Executive Survey 2021*. Boston: New Vantage Partners.

ONC [Office of the National Coordinator for Health IT] (2020). 21st century Cures Act: interoperability, information blocking, and the ONC Health IT Certification Program. Federal Register, August 4. https://www.healthit.gov/sites/default/files/cures/2020-03/ONC_Cures_Act_Final_Rule_03092020.pdf.

Optum (2020). Third annual Optum survey on AI in health care. https://www.optum.com/content/dam/optum3/optum/en/resources/ebooks/3rd-annual-ai-survey.pdf.

Strickland, E. (2019). How IBM Watson overpromised and underdelivered on AI in health care. *IEEE Spectrum*, April 2. https://spectrum.ieee.org/biomedical/diagnostics/how-ibm-watson-overpromised-and-underdelivered-on-ai-health-care.

Index

Titles in the **Elgar Advanced Introductions** series include:

International Political Economy
Benjamin J. Cohen

The Austrian School of Economics
Randall G. Holcombe

Cultural Economics
Ruth Towse

Law and Development
Michael J. Trebilcock and Mariana Mota Prado

International Humanitarian Law
Robert Kolb

International Trade Law
Michael J. Trebilcock

Post Keynesian Economics
J.E. King

International Intellectual Property
Susy Frankel and Daniel J. Gervais

Public Management and Administration
Christopher Pollitt

Organised Crime
Leslie Holmes

Nationalism
Liah Greenfeld

Social Policy
Daniel Béland and Rianne Mahon

Globalisation
Jonathan Michie

Entrepreneurial Finance
Hans Landström

International Conflict and Security Law
Nigel D. White

Comparative Constitutional Law
Mark Tushnet

International Human Rights Law
Dinah L. Shelton

Entrepreneurship
Robert D. Hisrich

International Tax Law
Reuven S. Avi-Yonah

Public Policy
B. Guy Peters

The Law of International Organizations
Jan Klabbers

International Environmental Law
Ellen Hey

International Sales Law
Clayton P. Gillette

Corporate Venturing
Robert D. Hisrich

Public Choice
Randall G. Holcombe

Private Law
Jan M. Smits

Consumer Behavior Analysis
Gordon Foxall

Behavioral Economics
John F. Tomer